Fiction of
Namita Gokhale
A Critical Study

Fiction of Namita Gokhale

A Critical Study

Vandana Bhagdikar

Prestige Books International

New Delhi

Published by
Prestige Books International
New Delhi 110060
email: prestigebooks@gmail.com

Associate Office
P.O. Box 2250, Sydney 2001

ISBN: 978-93-82186-59-5

Printed in India

Contents

Dedicated

to

my beloved parents

Late Mr. Gunwantrao B. Gujar & Mrs. Charulata Gujar

my in–laws

Late Dr. Krishnarao Bhagdikar & Mrs. Usha Bhagdikar

my lovely children

Nachiket and Niharika

Preface

Indian women novelists have enriched Indian English fiction by a creative release of feminine sensibility. Through the eyes of these women writers, one gets a glimpse of a different world, till now not represented in literature. So when I decided to take up research for my doctoral degree, I had a keen desire to work on some Indian women novelists writing in English. After pursuing number of writers I found that the fictional world of Namita Gokhale remains unexplored to some extent and also I was drawn towards her on account of her unique delineation of characters, significant experiments in fictional form and narrative techniques. Women clearly occupy the centre stage in her novels. They have attempted to carve a niche for themselves in the male-dominated society.

The first chapter traces the history of Indian English writing in general and writings of women writers in particular. The second chapter deals with the theme of empowerment of women and how Namita Gokhale has handled it in her fiction. The third chapter deals with Namita Gokhale's unforgettable association with the area at the foothills of the Himalayas. Her emotional attachment for nature, people and places as expressed in the novels is also highlighted. The fourth chapter focuses on the narrative technique adopted by the author to put forth her point of view. The fifth chapter highlights the skill of Namita Gokhale as a character painter and also brings out the sterling qualities of some of the major characters. The final chapter critically summarizes the arguments made in the earlier chapters and also asserts the status of Namita Gokhale as a contemporary woman novelist.

No task can be successfully accomplished without the support, motivation, guidance and co-operation from the people associated with it. I humbly take this opportunity to express my gratitude towards all those who have contributed in completing this project. First of all I express my obeisance to God for giving me strength to undertake this difficult task. I am deeply indebted to my parents my father Late Mr. Gunwantrao Gujar and my mother Mrs. Charulata for instilling in me the spirit of hard work. They are always a source of encouragement and motivation for me. My family is the pillar of strength for me. I do not find words which can truly express my feelings for my husband Mr. Vijay Bhagdikar, without whose, abundant and encouraging co-operation it would have been impossible to complete this work. My children Nachiket and Niharika who sustained my unavoidable indifference uncomplainingly during my research work deserve my loving thanks.

I acknowledge with profound gratitude the contribution of Dr. B.V. Moharil, the supervisor of my Ph.D. studies for his constructive suggestions and valuable guidance which paved the way for writing of this book. I express my thanks to Dr. Urmila Dabir, former Head of the Department (English) of my college, for her co-operation and constant motivation. Dr. Sonba Salve, my former colleague and presently Associate Professor, Department of English Literature, The English and Foreign Languages University, Hyderabad, needs a very special thanks. In fact he was instrumental in introducing me to Prof. R.K. Dhawan and also for his whole-hearted support and constant encouragement in completion of this book.

This acknowledgement would be incomplete without expressing my gratitude to my late father-in-law Dr. Krishnarao Bhagdikar who was always encouraging and supportive in all my academic endeavours. I humbly pay homage to his memory and seek his blessings for the success of my work. I am deeply indebted to my author Namita Gokhale for sparing her most valuable time to have a telephonic conversation whenvever I sought clarification regarding my research work. And finally I am indebted to Prof. R.K. Dhawan and Dr. Suman Bala of the University of Delhi. Had they not taken interest in its publication, this book would not have come out in its present form. Their valuable suggestions and quick response to my queries during the entire process of publication of this project helped me immensely. I am grateful to Prestige Books for bringing out this book so elegantly and expeditiously.

Nagpur **Vandana Bhagdikar**

Introduction

The creation of the Indian novel was an outcome of the influence of pre-independence Indian writing, especially in Bengali. Perhaps the first novel written in Bengali was *Alaler Gharer Dulal* which was published in 1858. However, the real beginnings were with the work of the great Bankim Chandra Chatterjee. His first published effort—*Rajmohan's Wife* (1864)—was in English. It was followed next year by *Durgeshnandini* in Bengali, which appeared in an English translation in 1890. *Kapalkundala*, *Vishavriksha* (The Poison Tree: A Tale of Hindu Life in Bengal), *Krishna Kantar Uyil* (Krishnakanta's Will), *Anandamath*, *Devi Chaudhurani* and other novels appeared between 1866 and 1886 and several of them came out sooner or later in English versions also. In the meantime, Raj Lakshmi Devi's *The Hindu Wife* was published in 1876, Toru Dutt's *Bianca* in 1878, Kali Krishna Lahiri's *Roshinara* in 1881, H. Dutt's *Bijoy Chand* in 1888 and Khetrapal Chakravarti's *Sarata and Hingana* (1895). These novels for us today have only historical importance.

Bankim Chandra Chatterjee wrote romantic as well as historical novels. In his historical novels, he was inspired by Todd's *Annals of Rajasthan* and Scott's historical romances. *Anandamath* (1882) is Bankim's best-known novel.

Rabindranath Tagore has written a considerable number of novels. Initially he wrote under the influence of Bankim Chandra. He achieved his first success with *Chokher Bali* (1902), now translated into English as *Binodini* by Krishna Kripalani. *Naukadubi* (1905) appeared as *The Wreck*, *Gora*

(1910) retained the same title in English also and *Ghare Bhaire* (1916) became *The Home and the World*.

If Tagore began, first by imitating Bankim and only then found his own voice, Sarat Chandra Chatterjee also went through a Bankim stage and Tagore stage of imitative writing before outgrowing them both in his best work in *Srikanta*, *Grihadara*, *Pather Dabe*, *Bipradas* and *Ses Prashna*.

The vicissitudes of the Bengali novel foreshadow more or less the vicissitudes of the novel in India. Before 1947, the English models were the major outside influence on the Indian novel. After independence, however, novelists in India have shown themselves susceptible to the influence of American and European models and also models from the Oriental countries. The novel in India, whatever its medium, is subject to the same or at least similar discontents and limitations. There are certain trends, which are found almost everywhere. The novelists either turn in nostalgia to the past and glorify and idealize it, or turn to the present in a gesture of protest if not disgust. After the advent of independence, the more serious novelist has shown how the joy of freedom has been more than neutralized by the tragedy of the partition; how in spite of the freedom there is continuing corruption, inefficiency, poverty and cumulative misery; how, after all, the mere replacement of the white sahib by the brown sahib cannot effect a radical cure for the besetting ills of India.

Pioneers like M.R. Anand, R.K. Narayan and Raja Rao depict the socio-economic and political realities of life in their novels. The nineteen thirties were the seed time of modern independent India, the Gandhian salt satyagraha movements of 1930 and 1932, the three Round Table Conferences, the passing of the Government of India Act of 1935, the introduction of provincial authority in 1937, the Gandhian movements for Harijan uplift and Basic Education, the organization of Marxist parties of diverse hues, the involvement in the war in 1939, the schism in the Congress leading to the expulsion of Subhash

Chandra Bose and his eventual escape to Germany and Japan—it was a decade full of activities.

Although, normally Anand resided in England yet he could not keep himself away from these developments which provided food for his novel writing. *Untouchable* (1935) covers the events of a single day in the life of the 'low caste' boy, Bakha. *Coolie* (1936) deals with the life of hill-boy Munoo, *Two Leaves and a Bud* (1937) may be said to be essentially a dramatic novel which culminates in a tragic clash of interests and destinies.

R.K. Narayan is one of the few writers in India who take their craft seriously, constantly striving to improve the instrument, pursuing with a sense of dedication what may often seem to be the marriage of technical perfection. Narayan published his first novel *Swami and Friends*, in 1935 which was received as a great work of art. His next novels *The Bachelor of Arts* (1937), *The Dark Room* (1938), *The English Teacher* (1945), *Mr. Sampath* (1949), *The Financial Expert* (1952) , *The Guide* (1958), *The Man Eater of Malgudi* (1961) and *The Vendor of Sweets* (1967) made him popular. *The Guide* won the prestigious Sahitya Akademi Award.

In Narayan's novels, there is generally a flight, an uprooting, a disturbance of order—followed by a return, a renewal, a restoration of normalcy. There are moments of heightened consciousness, marking a twist or a turn in the life of the people concerned. Such moments are often unexpected and they reveal the soul of the character. His novels are replete with simplicity, preciseness and inconsequential humour and pathos.

Raja Rao, a contemporary of Mulk Raj Anand and R.K. Narayan, makes with them a remarkable triad affiliated with them in time and sometimes in the choice of themes but not in his art as a novelist. His first novel *Kanthapura* (1938) portrays a most graphic, vivid and realistic account of the Gandhian freedom struggle in the 1930s and its impact on the masses of India. The tremors of Gandhi's impact on South-Indian village are recorded here in the chatty language of an elderly widow. *The Serpent and the Rope* was published after a gap of twenty-two years. Through this novel Raja Rao founded a new genre—the philosophical novel and forcefully realized the confrontation of eastern and western cultures. The novel is also regarded as the spiritual auto biography of the novelist. His third novel *The Cat and Shakespeare* (1965) is a philosophical comedy. It is marred by too much crudity and absurdity.

The tradition of social realism and new consciousness was further continued by Bhabani Bhattacharya, Manohar Malgonkar and Khushwant Singh. Bhabani Bhattacharya, a social realist, like M.R. Anand was highly influenced by the doctrine of Mahatma Gandhi and G.B. Shaw. His themes are close to social reality and based on real experience. He is concerned with large public issues and social problems. He generally writes about poverty, hunger, pestilence, traditionalism and the resulting controversy of Gandhian panacea versus rapid industrialization.

The novelists of this decade, especially the new and young ones are marked out by their obsession with their own generation and contemporaneity. New generation Indian English novels concentrate on the problems of contemporary youth—emotional, cultural, familial—and assess the present situation by looking back at the past. Another particular thing about the Indian novels is their Diasporic nature. Many novelists like Vikram Seth, Vikram Chandra, Shashi Tharoor, Amitav Ghosh, Gita Mehta and Amit Chaudhari are exploring the life in this country from afar. Others like Arundhati Roy are based in the metropolis of India and grapple with its life in their works.

New generation Indian English novelists are products of a sharply changing society that is undergoing marked transformation under the impact of globalization, media and cyber culture. Their novels are characterized by uninhibited narrative with no holds barred about sex, incest and registered strong antagonism of the socio-cultural mores and religious beliefs of earlier generation. They project the dilemma and expectations of the Indian youth—the relationship with parents, job-crisis, cultural alienation representing a generation in flux and unattached.

From time immemorial, Indian women, the embodiment of love and affection, hope and patience have been showing their worth in each and every discipline of knowledge. Gargi and Anusuya in scriptures, Sita and Rani Durgavati, Rajia Begum and Noorjahan in history and Mahasweta Devi and Manju Kapur, Ruth Prawer Jhabvala and Arundhati Roy and many more in fiction, have left their indelible imprint on the pages of history.

Indian women novelists in English deal with, apart from many other things, the pathetic plight of forsaken women who are fated to suffer from birth to death. She is a silent sufferer and is given secondary status both in the family and society. From time immemorial, attempts were made to redefine her identity in relation to man as wife, mother, daughter, sister but tradition trains a woman to think herself as an inferior being. She takes pride in suffering and lives with the idea of subjugation entrusted to them for years about the necessity to accept the rules assigned to them by patriarchy.

The history of Indian women novelists in English begins with Toru Dutt who died at the early age of 21, lesser than John Keats of the Romantic School of poetry. Both her novels—*Bianca* and *Le Journal Mademoiselleid'Arvers* deals with the autobiographical projections of the novelist's experiences which she gathered in her very short life. The story of Bianca and her sister Iniz and the story of Marguerite and sister Veronique are two separate attempts to tell the same inner tragedy of sisterly love and bereavement. But superimposed on this theme, there is in both novels the romantic love motif also, the understanding of which was largely drawn from literature while death was something she had seen. Though the characters are Spanish and

French, yet the delineation is entirely Indian, full of love and affection, sincerity and purity, which characterize the core of an ideal Indian woman.

After the Second World War women novelists got a new direction and vision and their quality work began enriching Indian fiction in English. Among these writers, Kamala Markandaya and Ruth Prawer Jhabvala are unquestionably the most outstanding personalities in the field of social and artistic novels.

In Kamala Markandaya's first novel, *Nectar in a Sieve* which has been compared with Pearl Buck's *The Good Earth* and K.S. Venkaramani's *Murugan the Tiller*, we find a typical Tamil Nadu village where life has apparently not changed for a thousand years. With the invasion of industry and modern technology in form of tannery arise sinister issues. The novel deals with a realistic picture of the Indian villagers, their customs and cultures, rites and traditions. The villagers or the downtrodden have to work night and day in their field to earn their living. They try their best to churn nectar from the ocean of their mother earth. But the irony is that the churned out nectar is bound to be placed in the sieve.

Kamala Markandaya's *Some Inner Fury*, is a tragedy engineered by politics, even as *Nectar in a Sieve* is a tragedy engineered by economics and in both novels the chief characters transcend the bludgeonings of economic or political mischance and assert the unconquerable spirit of humanity. *A Silence of Desire* of Kamala Markandaya unfolds the layers of spiritual reality and mystic vision of India. "Possession" (1963), is in a sense a continuation of *A Silence of Desire*. In her fifth novel, A *Handful of Rice* (1966), Kamala Markandaya avoids the disturbing extravagance of "Possession," extravagance in sense and situation. If the outer theme of *Nectar in a Sieve* was rural economics, the theme of *A Handful of Rice* is urban economics. *The Coffer Dams* (1969) is a fine blending of art and truth, feeling and form. It is a story of the British engineers who construct a river dam in Independent India.

The Nowhere Man deals with the theme of the anti-immigrant wave of the Sixties which engulfs the life of Srinivas, an old Indian widower and a Londoner who is persecuted mercilessly by a number of fanatics. In this novel the image of disease is very suggestive. The disease 'leprosy' suggests the protagonist's sense of isolation and disintegration.

Ruth Prawer Jhabvala has also left an indelible imprint in the history of women novelists in English. She was born of Polish parents in Germany and was educated in England but married an Indian and lived in India more than twenty-four years. Most of her writings deal with the various shades of Indianness, apart from many other things. Her novels ring the note of two things—urban middle-class Indian life tinged with domestic problems of an average joint Hindu family and ironic studies of the confrontation between occidental and oriental attitudes.

To Whom She Will presents a very beautiful picture of Indian society—its rites and customs, taste and temperament and above all marriage and love with an element of illicit relationships. This novel also deals with a truthful portrayal of the fatal consequences arising out of partition which uprooted millions of people. The Booker prize winning novel of R.P. Jhabvala, *Heat and Dust* deals with the sad and moving story of two English women who paid their visit to India and in return they became the victims of this country.

Nayantara Sahgal, the niece of Jawaharlal Nehru and daughter of Vijayalaxmi Pandit, is a novelist of politics. Her novels truthfully mirror the contemporary Indian political theme. Unlike other political writers she does not propagate any specific political ideology or favours any political creed or movement. Her novels portray the contemporary incidents and political realities saturated with artistic colour and objectivity. All major characters of her novels are centripetally drawn towards the vortex of politics. But besides politics, her fiction also focuses attention on Indian women's search for sexual freedom and self-realization.

Sahgal's first novel, *A Time to be Happy*, has references to Congress activities and the events of 1942. *This Time of Morning* is a purely political novel dealing with incidents occurring in the corridors of power, in the drawing rooms of the political figures. *The Day in Shadow* (1971) is also inspired by the political movement of the society. Although the main theme of the novel is politics, yet the problem of divorce and disintegration of the marriage in a typical Indian setting are also beautifully dealt with. *A Situation in New Delhi* (1977) deals with the Naxalite movement, student unrest and most importantly aftermath of Nehru's death. The novel shows that there is no gap between the private world and the political world; both the worlds are reciprocally treated in which actions and characters are co-mingled.

Ruth Prawer Jhabvala mirrors the social background in her works, Kamala Markandaya deals with the diverse contemporary problems—social, cultural, political—of the contemporary society in which the novelists grew up. Anita Desai deals with the inner working of the protagonists and unveils the hidden depths of human psyche. She represents the welcome 'creative release of the feminine sensibility' which began to emerge perceptibly on the literary horizon after the Second World War. Her forte is the quest of sensibility and her writing exposes inner realities and psychic echoes of her characters. Her novels present an explanation to the long-smothered wail of a lacerated psyche.

Anita Desai's maiden novel *Cry, the Peacock* (1963) presents an incompatible marriage of the protagonist, Maya. She is a spoiled and pampered daughter of a wealthy Brahmin and is married to Gautama, an older man, insensitive, pragmatic and rational lawyer who fails to understand her sensitive nature. The ever-widening gap in communication between the husband and the wife is felt throughout the novel. *Voices in the City* (1965) deals with an account of the odyssey of young women doomed to reside in Calcutta. Monisha's situation is a typical representation of the social situation of numerous young brides in India who, unable to bear endless torment and maltreatment from their husband's family members, end up as cases of bride-burning, suicide or self-immolation.

Where Shall We Go This Summer (1982) portrays the aching void in the life of Sita, by probing deeper into her life as a woman, a wife and a mother. Disaster stretches out from the very beginning of Sita's marriage to Raman, which is already tottering on the verge of collapse, when she runs away to her childhood home, in the hope of a miracle that would save her from giving birth to her fifth child in this violence-ridden world around her. The sense of alienation from her husband as an existential problem is greater in this novel than in the others.

Fire on the Mountain (1977) is basically the story of the agonized cries of Nanda Kaul and Ila Das. In *Clear Light of Day* Mrs. Desai portrays the development through the stream of consciousness of the two main characters, Bim (Bimla) and Tara, elder and younger sisters of Das family. In *Bye-Bye Blackbird* (1985) Sarah is presented as a sensitive and reserved person. She suffers when Adit, her husband, reveals the credulous side of his character to invite scorn and pity from her relatives, friends, colleagues and acquaintances.

Shashi Deshpande occupies a significant place among the contemporary women novelists who concern themselves with the problems of women and their quest for identity. Her first novel *Roots and Shadows* published after *The Dark Holds No Terrors* and *If I Die Today*, indicates the initial quest of woman for her self. The same quest is continued in her later novel *That Long Silence*.

In *Roots and Shadows*, the protagonist Indu is a middle-class young girl, born in an orthodox Brahmin family which is headed by Akka, the mother figure in the novel. Indu's mother had died at her birth but Akka identifies herself as a mother figure throughout the novel. She comes back after eleven years of her marriage, to her parental home on Akka's death and becomes inheritor of her property.

Saru in *The Dark Holds No Terrors* has childhood trauma. Her mother has gender difference in the treatment of her son Dhruva and her daughter. Saru hates her mother and rebels all her life. *That Long Silence* (1989) deals with the protagonist, Jaya's passage through a maze of self-doubts and fears towards the affirmation of her self. A crisis in the middle class family of the protagonist triggers off a chain of events which compel her to view her life in retrospection.

In *The Binding Vine* (1992), Deshpande uses the personal tragedy of the narrator-protagonist, Urmi to focus attention on victims like Kalpana and Mira—victims of man's lust and women's helplessness. The novelist makes a bold attempt to portray the agony of a wife who is the victim of marital rape, a theme which perhaps has not been touched upon by any other Indian writer in English. In *A Matter of Time* (1996), Deshpande liberates herself from the narrow confines of women and their problems and enters into the metaphysical world of philosophy.

Shashi Deshpande's novel, *Small Remedies* is the most confident assertion of her strength as a novelist with her deliberate denial of sentimentality and her total control over the unwieldy material, structured as a biography within a biography. It is about Savitribai Indorikar, the ageing doyenne of Hindustani music who does not marry in pursuit of her genius. It also tells the story of Leela who gives up her respectability in order to gain love and unhappiness in equal measure.

Shobha De is a modern novelist who is famous for portraying the sexual mania of the commercial world. In narrating the incident she is very frank and straightforward like Anita Desai. She has the gift of exploring the subdued depths of women psychology. In 1988, she shot into literary limelight by writing her first novel, *Socialite Evenings* which is Lawrencian in expression. *Starry Nights* also deals with the brazen portrayal of sex and sexploitation. Most of the characters in the book were based on actual individuals encountered by the novelist. In *Sisters* (1992), she presents the changing face of Indian woman. This woman is glamorous, capable, career-oriented, ambitious and successful.

Arundhati Roy, a novelist of world fame, won the prestigious Booker prize for *The God of Small Things*. The book is autobiographical in nature and deals with a pale reflection of the haunts of Roy's own childhood on the limpid back waters of Kerala and the society she lived with. The story revolves round the village, Ayemenem near Kottayam. The theme deals with the life of Keralite society, their rites and customs, tradition and patriarchal dealings, a caste-ridden mentality of some certain section of people; the fatal consequences arising out of divorce, the child psychology, the naked exposure of the malpractices of Marxism and police administration etc.

Namita Gokhale is also one of the famous novelists. She was born in 1956 in Lucknow. She spent her childhood between New Delhi and Nainital, in the foothills of the Himalayas. She was only 17 when in college in Delhi she met the Maharashtrian Rajiv Gokhale, son of Law Minister in Indira Gandhi's cabinet. Rajiv was merely two years older than her. They fell in love. She proposed to him and he accepted her proposal. Six months later they were married. As Indira Gandhi remarked at the wedding ceremony, it was like a marriage of two dolls.

Namita Gokhale also dropped out of college after a conflict over the bias against Indian literature in the curriculum. She along with her husband then published film magazine *Super* from Bombay.

Namita Gokhale by now had enough material to start writing a novel. In 1984 her first novel, *Paro: Dreams of Passion* was published. It was an instant success in India and abroad. It was a love story with erotic overtones. With this novel Namita Gokhale was well and truly launched. She began to collect material for her second book *A Himalayan Love Story*. While she was putting it into shape, she was stricken with cancer of the uterus. Rajiv rushed her to Bombay, for weeks her life hung by a single thread. Khushwant Singh, the famous writer who was closely associated with Namita Gokhale, was also unaware of her serious illness. He tells us: "I, who was among the people she kept in close contact with, knew nothing about it till a month ago. Namita Gokhale never looked for sympathy: it was only her inner resources, her 'survival strategy,' that helped her pull through the ordeal."[1]

This brush with death, however, left an indelible mark on her psyche. She had more experiences of death. Her mother-in-law died in her arms; her sister-in-law, Sunanda Bhandare, Judge of the Delhi High Court, succumbed to cancer and finally her husband Rajiv died in Singapore of cirrhosis of the liver, leaving Namita Gokhale to take care of their two teenage daughters. Despite tragedies in her personal life, she continues with her life with optimism. She is a religious person and prays everyday to derive strength particularly to Lord Hanuman. She finds in him a special combination of physical strength, mental agility and pragmatism. For her, the times of crisis are more defining and enriching. She expresses her opinions in an interview with Nadine Kreisber: "I actually consider those moments more defining and enriching than times of stability and happiness. Indeed, I find the latter quite debilitating as very few of us have the intelligence to use them for internal resources building, while at times of difficulty, everything in our nature pushes us to fight, to grow, to expand."[2]

Namita Gokhale has written six novels and two works of non-fiction, all in English. Her first novel *Paro: Dreams of Passion*, a satire upon the Mumbai and Delhi elite, was critically acclaimed and it caused an uproar due to its mischievous sexual humour. The novel deals with the story of an irresistible, tall, sexy, green-eyed temptress in the social whirl of New Delhi. Wandering through the world of privilege and decadence, Paro is observed constantly by Priya, the eternal voyeur and diarist who herself is in love with her boss, B.R., the sewing machine magnate. He is inevitably trapped by Paro into wedlock, but to Priya's discomfiture. The novel is presented as a confessional account of the narrator's own experience and those of her friend, Paro.

Her next novel *Gods, Graves and Grandmother* (1991) is a satire on present-day India. The novelist has skillfully strung different episodes like beads of a rosary to portray the seamier side of Indian life and morality. The novel deals with the story of a family of Kothawalis (prostitutes) once living in a large haveli and patronized by the rich zamindars, merchants and even the sahibs. Gudiya, her mother and Grandmother (Ammi) have to leave their Kotha. With no money, they find themselves on the road to destitution. Ammi is too old to be of service to her clients but still has a melodious voice to sing bhajans. Her daughter suddenly loses all her hair and elopes with a beggar who does not mind having a bald mistress. So the destitute grandmother and grand-daughter arrive in Delhi and set up a make-shift temple under the peepal tree and a hut to sleep in.

A Himalayan Love Story (1996) is the story of Parvati, young, beautiful and doomed, and Mukul Nainwal, the local boy groomed by the Headmaster, Hiranand Joshi. Mukul returns to Nainital of his youth to search for the only woman he has ever loved. The tale is told in the voices of Parvati and Mukul.

Gokhale's next novel, *The Book of Shadows* (1999) tells the story of a young university lecturer, Rachita, whose fiancé has killed himself. His sister considers her responsible for the incident and deforms her through an assault with acid. Rachita learns to handle her pain in a remote house in the Himalayan mountains, when the violent fate of its former inhabitants is played before her inner eyes. This grotesque and vividly narrated work has been compared to Isabel Allende's *House of Spirits*.

The book was an attempt by the novelist to find out about death. The ghost in the novel serves the purpose of exploring the soul's outward journey. She also experienced certain strange things while writing the novel. Namita Gokhale remembers: "While I was writing this novel, my computer behaved really strange. I had read that computers have a sensitive nervous system. When I was completing what was then the last draft of the novel, I overwrote the file. As soon as I realized this, I tried to retrieve it. But it had disappeared without a trace. Later, the blank computer screen showed the words: Hex 666. Now, Hex is just a computer program, but at that time, it looked pretty sinister. Then, without anybody touching any keys, these lines from the novel came upon the computer screen: 'I hide in corners, I lurk in shadows.' It was unnerving." [3]

Gokhale's novel, *Shakuntala: The Play of Memory* (2005) first appeared in Hindi translation before the English edition was published. The plot is inspired by the over thousand year old play *Shakuntala*, written in Sanskrit by the Indian poet Kalidasa. The story of a young woman who learns through a blind priest in Kashi about the mystery of her former life, which she must now come to terms with, plays with the recurring theme of memory and desire. It has been compared by more than one critic to Hermann Hesse's *Siddhartha*. Once again Gokhale links a woman's tragic love story to religion, the history of the country and philosophy. Arnab Bhattacharya opines about the book: "Gokhale's gripping and nuanced narrative offers a colourful template of ancient Indian life, rich in details of customs and rituals, faiths and fears, omens and superstitions. But the lyrical surface of her prose convulses, at times with the tensions and angst hidden underneath. Gokhale adroitly makes Shakuntala's yearning for the part of her self which takes her away from home (owned by her husband Srijan and shared by a housemaid, Kamalini, of whom she was jealous) contingent upon the gradual unfurling of an inward-turned Indian society." [4]

Gokhale's recent novel *Priya in Incredible Indyaa*, a sequel to the hugely popular *Paro: Dreams of Passion,* is a social comedy. Its easy and fluent prose parodies the glitterati of Delhi to perfection. Gokhale captures with élan the idiom of the city's super-elite—politicians, arms dealers, cricketers and what have you. It is one of those narratives where point of view makes all the difference. The narrative is in the form of diary entries by Priya, the wife of Suresh Kaushal, the Minister of State for Food Processing.

The novel traces the roller-coaster life of Priya, a girl from India's growing middle class, who works her way up through social and professional ranks to become the wife of an Indian minister, Suresh Kaushal. Priya copes with social vertigo, infidelity, menopause and relationships and learns some vital lessons watching her new friend Poonam chase status, sex and designer shoes. The novel is also a journey into the layered core of the country's changing economic scenario and the issues politicians strive to unravel in a flurry of five-star dos peopled by networkers, operators, business magnates and social hangers-on.

The author has also written two books of essays. *The Book of Shiva* (2001) is an erudite and impassioned examination of the Hindu god of death and regeneration and *Mountain Echoes* (1998) is a book of oral biography featuring the reminiscences of a generation of older women from the Kumaon Himalayas. She has also retold the Indian epic *Mahabharata* for young readers, to be published soon. In addition to her literary oeuvre, she is a director of Yatra Books, a recently established publishing company that co-publishes with Penguin Books in Hindi, Marathi and Urdu. She is currently working on a new novel, a generational saga titled *Things to Leave Behind* that examines continuity and change in the Indian subcontinent.

The 'Namita Gokhale' editions, a signature imprint published in association with Roli Books, introduced some notable titles including Rashna Imhasly Gandhy's *The Psychology of Love* and Neelima Dalmia Adhar's biography of her father, R.K. Dalmia. She has also conducted two memorable writers' retreats in Landour, with Roli Books, for the Namita Gokhale editions. She is committed to showcasing and translating the best of Indian writing and engaging the vibrant Bhasha languages of the Indian subcontinent in a creative dialogue with each other and the rest of the world.

Gokhale contributes regularly to several newspapers and magazines with focus on women's issues and current literary criticism. She also gives advice on bereavement in regular newspaper columns. Gokhale conceptualized the famous International Festival of Indian Literature, Neemrana 2002, and also The Africa Asia Literary Conference, Neemrana 2006. She is a co-director of the Jaipur Literature Festival for 2008 and 2009 and helped to design and programme the previous Jaipur Literature Festival of 2006 and 2007.

The experience of love and passion, illness and death, has shaped Gokhale's work as also her Kumaoni upbringing. For her, writing is a therapeutic experience. She observes: "Writing a novel is also a therapeutic experience. Human character and human destiny are formed by the way we handle our life crisis. When you write a novel, in hindsight, you realize that you were actually examining why you made certain choices. But, at the same time, writing is a neurotic activity. You build a parallel universe, you play God with your characters."[5]

Gokhale feels that everybody has two novels in him, one is the story of life as it is and another is the life as it might have been. After all, she has not had only good things happening to her. She has had her brush with adversity, and much of the pain emanating from the loss of near and dear ones has provided her with fuel to pen together some stories, some novels and some essays. She has always found writing 'a catharsis' and story-telling quite 'a therapeutic exercise.'

On being asked by Humara Quraishi about her personal life affecting her writing, she replied: "It's strange, but often I write about things before they happen to me or to those around me. I used to get terrified by these coincidences until a very intelligent woman explained to me that writers are intuitive and often carry a field of prescient energy, otherwise every writer I know cannibalizes experience, it's inevitable."[6]

Her bookshelves are lined with a confusing variety of books. Han Suyin's *Wild Swans* cohabit with Ouspensky's *Tertium Organum* and Kiran Nagarkar's *Cuckold*. But under her cosmopolitan manner, Gokhale's persona remains that of the Kumaoni Brahmin woman she is. The writer who grew up in Nainital remains obsessed by the air of the mountains. All her works seem to be stuck with her personality as a Kumaoni Brahmin girl. She accepts: "My way of looking at the world remains trapped in that primary identity, once you start loving the hills they hold on to you."[7]

The novels of Namita Gokhale reveal her keen concern for the welfare of women. In the chapters that follow, various facets of Namita Gokhale's novels are critically analyzed.

NOTES

1. Khushwant Singh, *The Tribune,* Oct. 30, 1999.
2. Namita Gokhale, interviewed by Nadine Kreisber, "Difficulty pushes us to fight, to grow," *Indian Express*, 22 July, 2007.
3. Namita Gokhale, on her book *The Book of Shadows*, http: //www.lifepositive.com.
4. Arnab Bhattacharya, "Bitter-Sweet Memories," *The Telegraph,* Calcutta: June 10, 2005.
5. Namita Gokhale, http: // www.lifepositive.com.
6. Namita Gokhale, interviewed by Humara Quraishi, "Every book has its life, its Kundali," *The Triubune,* Sept. 15, 2002.
7. Namita Gokhale, "Glimpses of Kumaon: An Overpowering Obsession with the Hills," *India Today*.

Empowerment of Women
An Overview

In the patriarchal cultural set-up the world over woman has been treated as the 'Object' or the 'Other' in relation to the male who constitutes the 'Subject.' She is desired, adored, glorified and also regarded as myth. She remains the passive recipient of the male's exuberant and passionate energy. Although she is physically and mentally equipped to perform on par with man, yet she has been denied existence as a complete human being. She is also deprived of the opportunity to give expression to her feelings, thoughts and anguish. She does not exist; she constitutes the absence while the male has presence. The dominant male strain in the society successfully puts woman in the background and consequently, shc is not allowed to foreground her ideas, joys, sorrows, likes and dislikes. She has been continuously and steadily suppressed and exploited by her man, the master who is at the centre of power. As Sushila Singh puts it: "Human experience for centuries has been synonymous with the masculine experience with the result that the collective image of humanity has been one-sided and incomplete. Woman has not been defined as a subject in her own right but merely has an entity that concerns man either in his real life or his fantasy life." [1]

The term 'feminism' has its origin in the Latin word 'femina' meaning 'woman' (through French 'feminisme'), and thereby refers to the advocacy of women's rights, status and power at par with men on the grounds of 'equality of sexes.' In other words, it relates to the belief that women should have the same social, economic and political rights as men.

Woman has always been projected as secondary and inferior. The bias against women can be seen rightaway from the day one of Creation. It is said that God created man in his own image. The suggestion is that God is male. Further, it is said that God, after creating man, made woman from the rib of man. As Adam, the first man on the earth, remarks about Eve: "This is now bone of my bones and flesh of my flesh, she shall be called woman, because she was taken out of man."[2]

The suggestion is that man is created first, and woman is taken out of man. In other words, woman is secondary to man. But the modern woman has raised her voice against the atrocity and injustice done to her. The new woman dares to pronounce her volitions and convictions. And it is their pronouncement in an overt tone that has created the difference in textuality.

It was mainly after the Women's Liberation Movement of the late 1960s that the contemporary feminist ideology evolved and the female voice was heard with special need. The focus of the literary studies was shifted to women's writing with a view to re-reading, revisioning and reinterpreting it in the light of long-existing gender bias and sexual politics in history, culture, society, family, language and literature.

Women's voices in literature have hardly been given due recognition and veneration. As John Singleton points out: "Women writers have in the past been categorized as either bitchy or gossipy. They shriek like harpies or they're trite and trivial."[3]

Feminism, thus, plays little or no part in the lives of most Indians. A few Indian writers in English have attempted to challenge the age-old myths surrounding the man-woman relationship. Some have succeeded in their attempt, if not in finding an ideal solution, but at least in creating awareness of the existing inequalities in society.

According to the historian Linda Gordan, feminism is "an analysis of women's subordination for the purpose of figuring out how to change it."[4] Women constitute roughly half the world's population, but their contribution in various fields of activity has been totally disproportionate to their numerical strength. Branded as the weaker sex, they have been denied full justice—social, economic and political.

The feminist movement which started in the west in the 1960s went a long way in arresting the injustice meted out to women. The term 'Feminism' was first used by the nineteenth century French dramatist, Alexander Dumas to refer to the-then emerging movement for women's rights which was mostly limited to politics. It gradually spread across the world, securing complete rights for women—political, social, economic and educational. The term became popular from the early twentieth century struggles for securing women's suffrage or voting rights (the suffragette movement) in the western countries and the later well-organized socio-political movement for women's emancipation from patriarchal oppression.

The genesis of feminism can be marked during the last decade of the eighteenth century when struggle for women's rights began. Mary Wollstonecraft's *A Vindication of the Rights of Women* (1797) is the most significant work concerning the quest for recognition of women's socio-cultural and political rights. Other prominent works dealing with such quests include Margaret Fuller's *Woman in the Nineteenth Century* (1845), John Stuart Mill's *The Subjection of Women* (1869) and Fredrich Engle's *The Origin of the Family* (1911). In the twentieth century the struggle was carried forward by suffragette movement.

In 1929, Virginia Woolf's book *A Room of One's Own* came to light and became the most important feminist document. She questioned, quite discreetly and self-consciously, why woman's space in literature was so limited. In her essays, as in

'Professions for Women,' she took up issues concerning women writers who were confined to the angel-in-the-house ideology of 'womanhood,' suffered from economic and socio-cultural disadvantages in the male-governed society and could not speak boldly about their experiences as a body under pressures of patriarchy. Another noteworthy work was Dorothy Richardson's stream of consciousness novel 'Pilgrimage.'

In the post-war period, Simone de Beauvoir's book, 'The Second Sex' which was first published in French in the year 1949 and later translated in English is an important landmark in the evolution of the feminist theory. She draws heavily on various disciplines like biology, psychology and history to express her ideas clearly. She studies in detail issues like girl's education, marriage, prostitution and domestic chores which she describes as unpaid drudgery. She frankly discusses the topics which were considered hitherto taboo—sexual initiation and sexual pleasure for women.

Beauvoir's book was a critique of literature so far shaped by men, especially with regard to the portrayal of women by the male writers such as D.H. Lawrence. She found that most of men's representation and interpretation of women's life and nature contained hidden male bias. She opined that woman is not feminine by birth, but she is made so by importunate process of socio-cultural conditioning: "One is not born, but rather becomes a woman. No biological, psychological or economic fate determines the figure that the female presents in a society, it is civilization as a whole that produces this creature which is described as feminine." [5]

Though Beauvoir's book sowed the seeds for a revolution, it did not exactly initiate the Women's Movement. It was Betty Friedan's 'The Feminine Mystique' published in 1963 which sparked off the movement. Friedan interviewed her erstwhile classmates fifteen years after graduating from college. Most of the women interviewed by Friedan were wives and mothers blessed with all the comforts of life yet the survey proved that they were merely playing the role of devoted wife and loving mother and were supposed to seek fulfillment in it. This survey proved that the general assumption of a woman achieving happiness and contentment in marriage and motherhood was false. Friedan holds the view: "For a woman, as for a man, the need for self-fulfillment—autonomy, self-realization, independence, individuality, self-actualization is as important as the sexual need, with as serious consequences when it is thwarted. Woman's sexual problems are in this sense, by-products of the suppression of her basic need to grow and fulfill her potentialities as a human being, potentialities which the mystique of feminine fulfillment ignores."[6]

Friedan's book was followed by Kate Millett's *Sexual Politics* in 1963. Millett is considered to be another important feminist of the twentieth century. She vociferously argues that in the patriarchal society, woman has been accorded a demeaning position. She gives a graphic explanation of the insecurities faced by woman and she anticipates the problem which society would face one day in the form of female foeticide with the result of rapid scientific development which would enable pre-natal sex determination tests.

The women's movement also produced a number of feminist novelists. Sylvia Plath's 'Bell Jar' took American women by storm. The novel depicts the transformation of the young, innocent and oppressed heroine, Esther, into a vengeful Diana. The novelist uses the exquisitely handcrafted mat made by Mrs. Willard, one of the characters, to symbolize the oppression of women. This mat is not used for interior decoration as some object of art but rather as a kitchen mat to be soiled under the feet of Mr. Willard.

Other feminist novelists in the west like Margaret Drabble, Doris Lessing, Iris Murdoch, Marilyn French and Margaret Atwood have created a niche for themselves in the literature produced in this century. They have come a long way from the constraints faced by their counterparts two hundred years ago. Women in those days did not dare defy the norms laid down by society on one hand while on the other men were permitted to ignore social decorum. It was expected that women writers should restrict themselves only to certain areas of life.

Society has undergone a see change since then. Women writers no longer have to assume pseudonyms, as in the case of George Eliot, to shield their identity. Women writers today enjoy a relatively greater freedom and do not shy away from exploring the domains which were earlier considered taboo. They are a lot more stridently feminist in their approach. India was also becoming aware of the changing trends of the west regarding their approach towards woman.

The thirties were the decade in which three founding fathers of modern Indo-Anglian literature, Raja Rao, R.K. Narayan and Mulk Raj Anand brought out their first novels. Their early novels gave a comprehensive vision of a society in which women were allocated a definite place. In the thirties women lived through a difficult time as they had to face two major contradictions. On one hand they had to play the part assigned to them by the holy text and on the other they were involved in the great reform movement of the day in which many of them assumed nation-wide responsibilities. The age-old respect for the laws of Manu still dictated the position of women within the family. A woman could not be independent and was meant to spend her life under the authority of a man: father, husband or brother in case of widowhood

Anand's protagonist Gauri in *The Old Woman and the Cow*, however, is a fine example of the idea of women's emancipation. Some of Narayan's women characters have also tried to assert themselves in their desire for a career or their need for physical gratification. In Bhabani Bhattacharya's novels, woman is the epitome of all virtues and plays an important role in bringing about social reform. But in spite of being pure and noble, she is victimized.

The women writers have realistically portrayed the women in their novels. They have been able to create interesting personages who successfully expose the oppression inflicted on women in society. They have indulged in exploring the feminine consciousness of the women characters, their evolution towards an awakened conscience and how eventually this leads to enrichment of their inner self in a male dominated society. Self-introspection and self-discovery help the women characters to realize their veiled inner strength.

It is to be remembered that the tradition of feminism whether Western or Eastern aims at improving the lot of women.

Many women novelists have dealt with the problems and difficulties faced by their women characters. Writers like Kamala Markandaya, Anita Desai, Shashi Deshpande, Nayantara Sahgal, Shobha De, Namita Gokhale, Gita Mehta, Uma Vasudev, Bharati Mukherjee etc., aimed at catching the whole woman alive in the terms of feeling, intellect and emotions. Their major concern has been the Indian woman's search for identity by setting her against her milieu. Though they write in English, these writers very skillfully and successfully capture the Indian ethos. At the same time, they show their deep insight into human nature, and their understanding of day-to-day problems.

The novels of Anita Desai are basically female oriented. She probes into the problems of her characters. She writes of the woman as a victim in a patriarchal, patrilineal and father-dominated Indian family. The Indian woman is forever, dominated by and dependent upon the male member of her family—be it the father, the brother, the husband, or the son. These are the various phases of an Indian woman's life and the novelist sharply focuses upon the emotional reactions of the woman as she experiences these stages. The women characters sometimes show an attitude of compromise and at times they rebel and gather sufficient courage to speak out a word of resistance. She depicts the Indian woman as a fighter, a victim, a heroine and ultimately a winner because of her indomitable spirit and attitude of compromise. She has portrayed both kinds of women—those who are symbols of growth and change and those who are symbols of withdrawal, regression, decay, death and destruction.

Shashi Deshpande's novels reveal the women's quest for self, an exploration into the subtleties of the human mind and society. She lays emphasis on the working of the psyche of her women characters, which plunge into a period of psychic disturbance due to traumatic experience of life. Their sufferings lead to a stage of self-introspection and later self-discovery which evinces a fresh perception of life. Ultimately her characters come out of the crisis as strong women willing to compromise with life as it comes.

Shashi Deshpande's *Roots and Shadows* depicts the agony and suffocation experienced by the protagonist Indu, in a male-dominated and tradition-bound society. In *That Long Silence*, the novelist portrays the plight of Jaya, the protagonist.

Nayantara Sahgal, another prominent Indian woman writer, began writing before the feminist movement was launched in the sixties. Yet in her novels she dealt with problems faced by women. She writes sensitively of the way women suffer owing to sexist bias in a patriarchal set-up. Sahgal's feminist ideas are restricted to a limited world. She restricts herself to the study of women of one class, the elite. She depicts the sufferings of these and shows how they refuse to remain chained to their subordinate roles and how they defy traditional norms in search of emancipation.

Like other novelists, Shobha De has focused in most of her novels, on the marginalization of women in Indian society. As a feminist novelist, she has marvelous understanding of the psyche of women and, therefore, she explores the world of especially urban woman with all its problems and challenges in her novels like *Socialite Evenings*, *Starry Nights*, *Sultry Days* etc.

Arundhati Roy's *The God of Small Things* deals with many feminist issues like women's deprivation of property rights, of equal human status and more. Roy presents three generations of doubly marginalized women: first by their binding native culture and secondly by the dominant forces of patriarchy. Namita Gokhale's novels, also present women characters in the Indian social set-up and their varied responses to society. She has depicted the problems and difficulties faced by her characters and have shown how they tackle these adverse situations.

Her first novel *Paro: Dreams of Passion* is a tale of a tall, sexy, green-eyed, gin-drinking temptress, Paro and is narrated by the observant Priya, who records not only the loves and failures of her friend but also her own. The basic theme of Paro is human predicament; it is a woman's agonizing search for her true self in the society which is still largely traditional and still dominant with cultural and societal stereotypes. Paro is the child of middle-aged parents. She spends her childhood in the hostel of a remote public school. She is sexually abused by a school teacher while in her teens, and this experience leaves an indelible scar on her psyche. As she tells Priya with tears in her eyes: "He raped me in a grove of pine-trees," she said, tears in her eyes. "He sodomized me in the woods behind the chapel. I still have the water colour I was painting when that happened, it shows the landscape exactly as it was the day my life began to get fucked up. You know, birds, butterflies, blue skies, the works. As it hangs in my bedroom. I look at it and weep." (29-30)

Paro was expelled from the school after being found with the art master. Her parents could not bear the shame. Consequently her father retired early and they shifted to Delhi. This experience paves the shortest and easiest way for Paro to rise above her middle-class background by exploiting her own sexuality.

Later on Paro gets married to B.R., the sewing machine tycoon. Soon after her marriage, she discovers B.R. with their neighbour's daughter. This horrifies her and she makes a suicide bid by wounding her wrist. But this evokes no reaction in B.R. This is the moment when Paro takes a momentous decision: "After that, I decided I would pay him back in his own coin. I mean, every one was in love with me, and who do you think could ever love that guy?" (59)

Priya, the narrator of the novel, was B.R.'s secretary. She presents a different aspect of woman's voyage to self-identification. Coming from a typically middle-class family she is mesmerized by the charm and sophistication of B.R. and is ashamed of her middle-class conditions. She vows to liberate herself from the tardy, shoddy and tedious middle class suburban existence. She dreams of grace and beauty: "I would awake disoriented in our small all purpose hall-cum-dinning-room, suffused with shame and contempt for the poverty and meanness around me. I would vow to rise from that mire; I would dream of grace, of beauty, and harmony and I would resolve to brush my hair a hundred strokes every night before I slept." (14)

Priya is also fascinated by Paro, with whom B.R. gets married. She wrote about Paro and B.R. because she sees herself in Paro. The fact that Paro snatches away B.R., with whom Priya herself has had a sexual liaison, is a hurt that Priya can neither forget nor forgive. She always wished that she were able to speak and act like Paro. Priya is dazzled by the bold beauty and reckless charm of Paro and longs for the grace, beauty and harmony represented by her. In comparison she feels crushed, beaten and defeated, and immediately puts Paro in the citadel of a rival. Priya thought that in order to get victory over her, she is to be imitated and outsmarted.

Ammi in *Gods, Graves and Grandmother,* who is narrator Gudiya's grandmother, runs a kotha or brothel. As is usual with kothewalis or courtesans, she becomes implicated in a murder case and is forced to leave her comfortable kotha along with her daughter and granddaughter. The narrator's mother, who had contracted a venereal disease, runs away with the beggar, Riyasuddin Rizvi, whom they meet at the Jhansi railway station. The grandmother along with her granddaughter reaches Delhi and they are left to look after themselves. Ammi, once a rich kothewali with a big haveli of hundred and thirty rooms, finds herself on the streets of Delhi. Gudiya describes their condition: "When my mother went away, my grandmother and I were left to fend for ourselves. I had always been given to believe that we had once been enormously rich, but at that time we were on the very verge of penury." (1)

Another character in the novel is of Phoolwati, who used to live in a village, while her husband, Shambhu, runs a tea shop in the same slum, where Ammi lives. He has an affair with Magoo, the labourer at the construction site. He is murdered by Magoo's husband, Saboo along with her. Widowed Phoolwati comes to Delhi for the funeral of her husband. She is all alone in the vast city of Delhi with no acquaintances. Ammi, Gudiya and Phoolwati thus come to a place which is completely new to them. They have to struggle to survive.

Parvati, the central character of *A Himalayan Love Story,* is a frail, poor and neglected daughter of a poor, neglected widow growing in one of the most backward areas of U.P. After her mother's death she comes to stay with her mother's brother Hiranand, the Headmaster at Wee Nooke in Nainital. He marries her off to one of his students, Lalit Joshi, who is a homosexual. He is hostile towards Parvati thus leading to an unsuccessful married life. Lalit is indifferent towards Parvati's needs and desires. Later on, Lalit dies of tuberculosis leaving Parvati pregnant with his brother's child.

Gokhale's *The Book of Shadows* presents the problem faced by Rachita Tiwari, the English literature teacher. Her fiancé, Anand commits suicide as he feels that she has betrayed him by yielding to persuasion of her friend's husband. Anand's sister throws a beaker full of acid on Rachita's face the day after inquest. Her face is disfigured as a result. She narrates painfully the incident:

> I had encountered her as I was re-contouring the shadow on my eye in the misty mirror in the bogs next to the cafeteria. There's a separate dressing room for staff and faculty upstairs, but I didn't want to face the other teachers. This was my first day in college after Anand's death. I saw her in the mirror, her face almost at my shoulder, and turned around in a vague panic. And then it happened. As my vision blurred, as my consciousness dissolved in a river of searing pain, I could hear the tinkle of her bangles, glass against gold, and the swish of her starched cotton sari as she walked, but leaving me alone in the toilet block." (5-6)

The acid attack causes an unbearable pain to Rachita. The acid had an impact on her bone cartilage and the surgeons tried to restore it to some extent. But in spite of that her face is disfigured and changed. She is left heart-broken and humbled and with little traces of what she used to look earlier. She now covers her face with long muslin chunni to hide her scarred face. With the pain of disfigurement, Rachita goes to the Himalayan retreat of Ranikhet.

Shakuntala, the central character and narrator of the novel *Shakuntala: The Play of Memory*, has the quest for experience and knowledge. She grew up in a mountain country under harsh conditions. Her father died when she was just five years old. He was a vaidya and her mother had learnt a little from him about healing. She had an elder brother Govinda, who was destined to become the man of dharma. Shakuntala did not want to become like her mother for she was restless to see the world, to wander with the freedom of birds and clouds, although her mother cautioned her against it. Shakuntala realized that her mother was more inclined towards her brother. When her brother along with his guru comes to visit their house, her mother is so engrossed in the hospitality that she completely ignores Shakuntala. At that time Shakuntala is bestowed with womanhood and her mother dragged her to the low stoop beside the cowshed and closed the door. It dawns upon her that she had been abandoned. An anger and helplessness rose within her:

> Even if I burst my lungs screaming, she would not hear me, my mother. An anger that had the feel and texture of helplessness rose within me, and I heard a scream emerge from some deep recess in my stomach. The sound fluttered like a torn pennant, defeated already in its purpose. I had been abandoned, I would bleed to death while my brother and his proud guru were plied with jaggery sweets. (31)

Shakuntala is married to Srijan, a Mahasamant, who was a rich man and the chief of fourteen villages. He would often undertake journeys to far off places for his work. He returns with a woman after one of his travels. This creates a sense of jealousy in Shakuntala and she is filled with rage and anger. She is hurt by the betrayal:

> But the hurt and betrayal, the prickling of thorns under the sheath of my skin—I had never known or anticipated these feelings, just as I had never expected my husband to return from his journey to the east with an exotically beautiful woman with cold and mocking eyes. (58)

These then are the problems and difficulties which stare women in the face. Anita Desai, Shashi Deshpande, Nayantara Sahgal, Shobha De, Arundhati Roy and Namita Gokhale have highlighted the plight and struggle (many times abortive) of the women in their novels.

Indian woman today is trying to break away from the ideals of Indian womanhood. Exposed to the western concept of liberated, independent individual, the woman in India too is on her journey of transformation from the timid, dependent and dumb person to a self-asserting, self-confident individual. She wants to bestir herself to shake off the sloth of centuries which thwarts her personality.

Paro: Dreams of Passion is essentially the story of an irresistible and passionate, though outrageous, woman of the same name. The novelist seems to have chosen characters like her precisely because they are psychologically more plausible and interesting. Then, there are strong reasons for such development as these characters take. Right from the beginning of the novel, Paro is presented as a proud, audacious and self-confident, ambitious woman "with an assured cat like grace." (10-11) The daughter of a retired Brigadier, she grew in due course into "so exotic a creature" (10) endowed with ravishing sensual looks. The only child of middle-aged parents, she became "a bother in their well-ordered lives." (30) While in boarding school, she had an affair with the art master and was consequently expelled from the school. In college she met B.R. who fell for her "like a ton of bricks!" (32) These two incidents changed the very course of her life.

Even a casual perusal of the novel impress upon the reader certain glaring qualities of Paro's character. She is so egocentric that "she loved her body and cried like a baby at the slightest physical hurt" (33) and "she would talk on, compulsively, about herself, always herself." (29) In her ambition, she wanted to be the Prime Minister of India. Two other factors which made her what she was are: her frightening irreverence and her excessive greedy vitality.

Thus, we see that, in *Paro*, Namita Gokhale emerges as a committed feminist author. She has successfully portrayed the insensitive fatality of option which the society has cringingly given to its women. Even though she is unable to develop a decisive stand on these issues, she has successfully recorded and documented the hopes and fears, the concerns and tensions of the contemporary educated woman and therein lays the success of the novel.

Ammi in *Gods, Graves and Grandmother* shows her strength when she is required to deal with Sundar Pahalwan who assumes that he is the owner of the pavement which is used by her for her Jhuggi. In her usual honeyed-voice, Ammi tells Sundar Pahalwan: "Seize our money, Pahalwanji but spare our self-respect. I am the widow of a Brahmin, my husband was a priest, guard your tongue or else a virtuous woman's curses may follow you!" (12)

The Pahalwan is further asked to come the following week and take his 'cash.' But the following Monday Sundar Pahalwan is surprised to find Ammi singing a bhajan, in front of 'a statue of Durga astride a tiger under a 'glittering canopy' with a band of worshippers assembled around the shrine. The result is Sundar Pahalwan is completely overpowered and he does not leave the shrine before leaving eleven rupees in the 'Thali.' Similarly, when the man from the Municipal Corporation comes with the demolition order for the 'pucca cement structure' which now houses Ammi and Gudiya, he falls at Ammi's feet and begs her forgiveness for the 'blasphemy.' This event shows that Ammi asserts herself tactfully.

Thus, we notice that Gokhale effects a paradigm-shift in the position of her women who are autonomous and do not depend for their survival, as Manu postulates, on their fathers, husbands or sons. They have the requisite strength to face life with all its ups and downs; they are sharply etched out in terms of their self and identity. They are cast in the mould of the New Woman who solves her problems herself and is assertive, practical and resilient. This image of the New Woman constitutes a forceful and effective rebuttal to the definition of woman as 'a sweetheart, a paramour, a mistress,' in most of the dictionaries. This significant work of fiction is in sharp contrast to several novels which end with 'madness, death, suicide, surrender' of the female protagonists. In her book Gokhale creates a female space which her women occupy with dignity, confidence and feeling of self-worth.

The female characters in the novels of Namita Gokhale face many problems and difficulties but they make an attempt to assert themselves. They try to break away from the shackles of patriarchal social set-up as it poses hindrance in their development. The ways adopted by them may vary but the aim is the same, i.e. to emancipate themselves.

Through the centuries woman in Hindu tradition is depicted as a silent sufferer. She has been given a secondary status both in the family and society. From time immemorial, attempts were made to redefine her identity in relation to man as wife, mother, daughter, sister but the tradition trains a woman to think of herself as an inferior being. In spite of the fact the women constitute at least one half of human race, woman is made to believe that this secondary position is not imposed of necessity by natural 'feminine' characteristics but rather by strong environmental forces of social tradition and education which have been under the control of men.

Indian women take pride in suffering and live with the idea of subjugation entrusted to them for years or in inculcation about the necessity to accept the roles assigned to them by patriarchy that runs through their blood. As Alladi Uma observes: "Subtle indoctrination atrophies a women's desire to change her position as an object and to exercise her free will; she compromises her stand, for she is taught the importance and necessity of a stable marriage and family—family as security, as a source of emotional strength."[7]

In a male-dominated society, woman is supposed to be an ideal wife, a mother and an excellent homemaker with multifarious roles in the family. As wife and mother, service, sacrifice, submissiveness and tolerance are her required attributes. She has to make a series of adjustments, yet she is not an equal to man. At every stage of her life, she has to be dependent for her status and survival upon man—her father, her husband, her son. Submissive, domesticated, unprotesting and self-sacrificing woman was an essential adornment of the patriarchal social set-up all over the world. In the Indian social milieu, in the lower stratum of society, woman is accustomed to beating by their drunkard husband. Namita Gokhale in her novels has portrayed women who try to break the set traditional norms.

Paro, in *Paro: Dreams of Passion* is shown to be a rebel who revolts against the social and moral codes assigned to a woman. As Kuldeep Kumar and Gajendra Kumar point out: "She is neither chaste nor submissive as is expected of a woman. She denies social codes, traditions, authority and all those things which force a woman to become a prisoner of her own sex."[8]

In the beginning of the novel we are told by Priya how Paro behaves in an untraditional manner at her marriage party. She did not at all resemble any traditional Indian bride. A bride is expected to keep her head downcast covered with sari pallav but Paro did not behave like a traditional bride. As Priya tells us: "She circulated through the room with an assured catlike grace. One mehndied hand carelessly held on to horror of horrors, a glass of gin! The other was graciously bestowed on B.R., who followed in her ake, a slightly glazed look, in his fine eyes." (10-11)

She does not behave with her father-in-law like a traditional bahu. At her wedding reception instead of touching her father-in-law's feet she greets him with "Hi, Daddyji." She also calls him, "That old lech." Her way of getting herself dressed up was also non-traditional. Unlike traditional Indian woman who is wrapped in a sari, she preferred wearing dresses: "She was wearing a black sequined off-shoulder kurta, which left one shoulder completely bare, almost naked to my prudish eyes." (22) Priya also tried to follow Paro and behaved in an untraditional manner. She would visit beauty parlours to change her outer look and wore modern dresses. She also started smoking to which Suresh, her husband, objected.

Gokhale's female characters display sexual autonomy which is again an attribute against tradition. They establish relationship with men before their marriage and lose their virginity. They even become pregnant before marriage which is unconventional. Paro, after her marriage to B.R., leaves him and starts living with 'Bucky' Bhandpur, a test cricketer and scion of a princely family. She leaves him and has a son of ambiguous parentage. Thus, she denies the social and moral codes and dares to have a child whose father is unknown. Later on she has relationship with a young boy called Avinendra, who is the son of the Industry Minister. He considered Paro to be a free woman, a real individual. As Priya tells us: 'She was now the free woman, symbol and prototype of emancipation and individuality. "I am myself," she said theatrically, "and no one else. I depend on nobody. I am my own person."' (48)

She also establishes relationship with a politician Shambhu Nath Mishra, the ugliest person Priya ever encountered. After a brief affair with him, she gets married to a gay European film director Loukas Learos. She also develops relationship with Priya's husband, Suresh. Paro seeks her identity in sexual freedom.

Veena Singh compares her with Gustav Flaubert's Madam Bovary, D.H. Lawrence's Lady Chatterley and Herman Hesse's Kamla. She writes: "Like Gustav Flaubert's Madam Bovary, D.H. Lawrence's Lady Chatterley and Herman Hesse's Kamla, Paro symbolizes female will. She is possessed with restlessness. She represents a woman who yearns for completion and who refuses to be consumed by the monstrous schematization of the male-dominated institution."[9]

The shortest and the easiest way for Paro to rise above her middle-class background is through exploiting her own sexuality. The knowledge that her body is something which she can put to use comes to Paro as a teenage girl when she is raped by her art master, the act she liked. It is a disgrace to her family, but to Paro it comes as triumph over her family. This is something like an immature and middle-class version of Karuna's declaration in Shobha De's *Socialite Evenings*, "I am the good thing." Karuna is mature and clever enough to turn her experience into a successful item for the media. Paro also uses her sexuality to achieve success in life. Her sexual exploits are the expression of "the free woman, symbol and prototype of emancipation and individuality," (48) a person dependent on nobody—being her "own person." Ferheize Bharucha compares this search to establish one's sexuality with a search for creativity: "When creativity in Art is not possible for her, Paro seeks an expression of creativity through sexual license—creativity herein being the charting out of her own definition of a dilettantish course of life."[10]

Paro's sexual exploits can be compared with Aasha Rani's in Shobha De's *Starry Nights* who is forced into the film industry by her mother. To become a successful star, she develops relationship with a number of men. Priya, from *Paro: Dreams of Passion*, also has relationship with B.R. before marriage as well as after her marriage. She has no guilt about her sexual encounter with B.R. but at the same time she is careful to keep her marriage intact. The same strategy is used by Indu from Shashi Deshpande's *Roots and Shadows* whereby she has no guilt about her sexual encounter with Naren but decides not to tell Jayant about it. Marriage fails to provide them the promised happiness. Priya's description of her second brief stint with B.R. in Bombay explains her ecstatic state: "I would meet B.R. almost every evening and have dinner with him, with wine, candlelight, roses and all the other trappings of a covert romance. We would make love in anonymous hotel rooms. I would punctuate his appointments and draft short memos of passion in his absence." (39)

Gudiya in *Gods, Graves and Grandmother* also develops relationship with Kalki before marriage. Parvati in *A Himalayan Love Story* has a brief sexual encounter with her history teacher, Salman before marriage. After marriage, as her husband fails to perform his marital duties, she develops relationship with Lalit's brother Raju who impregnates her with his child. Both Priya and Parvati are not guilty about their relationships. As P. Ramamoorthy observes: "Their sexual situation forces these women to extra-marital relationship. What is significant about such relationships is that they suffer no guilt and they begin to evolve a new code of sexual ethics. Their path to individuation is marked by contacts with diverse experiences such as extramarital affairs. They experience a sense of sexual autonomy freeing themselves from sexual politics."[11]

Rachita in *The Book of Shadows* has an affair with her friend's husband which consequently results in suicide of her lover Anand. Shakuntala in *Shakuntala: The Play of Memory* runs away with a Greek horse merchant in pursuit of knowledge and experience after her marriage to Srijan. All these women characters seek sexual autonomy in pursuit of self-assertion. They also consider marriage as an escape from prevalent conditions. Paro's marriage with B.R. is an escape from her middle-class background. So is the case with Priya, for her the standard Herald car decides her marriage with Suresh. As she tells us: "A photograph also spilled out, of an owlish youth leaning on a Standard Herald Car. The car decided me. From then on I was caught in a whirl of feverish planning and anticipation: all before I had even encountered my future husband, or he had met or approved me." (20)

Priya also takes to writing a diary about 'passion, boredom, vanity and jealousy.' It provides an escape route to her. It is her confession as well as catharsis. Monisha in Anita Desai's *Voices in the City* also writes a diary which acts as an outlet to her oppressed feelings. Towards the end of the novel when Suresh finds out about the relationship of his wife and B.R. through Priya's diary, she does not feel repentant at all. She minces no words in declaring that what she has written about B.R. and herself was fully true and not a figment of her imagination. She also honestly tells Suresh that she never had any real sentiment for him. The resultant separation between Priya and Suresh also does not make Priya repentant for what she had done. What Priya does in her marital life qualifies her to be called an emancipated modern woman who has shed some of the inhibitions imposed on a woman in the male-made social order.

Gudiya in *Gods, Graves and Grandmother* falls in love with Kalki, the bandwallah. She modifies the model in which man as the 'subject' seeks woman, the 'object' or the 'other.' The novelist creates a situation where a girl desires a boy. Gudiya is made the 'subject' and Kalki the 'object.' According to Subhash Chandra, this is reversal of the position. He says: "This conspicuous reversal of the polar positions between woman and man forms part of the conscious attempt on the part of novelist to displace male from the unquestionable dominant position he has occupied in the patriarchal system in which woman is considered 'forward' or lacking in womanly grace, if she desires a male, as a male does a female."[12]

Another significant aspect of Gudiya's personality is her desire to shed the childishness associated with her name. She does not like her name Gudiya. She decides to change her name: "I resolved to change my name, my identity my very self. I became a creature of possibilities unfettered by a past, totally involved in the process of becoming. All I lacked was a name." (127)

She changes her name to a royal sounding new name—Pooja Abhimanyu Singh. The change of her name is indicative of her attempt to carve out a new identity in society and acquire a self-worth. It is noteworthy that the feminists have always stressed upon self-worth and women empowerment which they feel will remove the feeling of inferiority in women. Gudiya proves the worth of her new name when she deals with the money-minded Mr. Lamba, husband of Mrs. Roxanne, in whose school she studied and Cyrus, Roxanne's nephew. According to the will left by Mrs. Lamba, Gudiya is left with a sizeable portion of her wealth. She opts out of the possibility of acquiring wealth in a dignified manner, thus belittling the two men.

Here the novelist seems to suggest that women are bestowed with higher qualities of generosity and selflessness. Another incident of her generosity is seen when she gives her jewellery to Kalki to enable him to go to Bombay in order to try his luck in the film world. Gudiya's support to Kalki is similar to Nisha's support to Deb in Shobha De's *Sultry Days* until he gets a job or starts earning. Here we find the reversal of situation where by a husband is supposed to support his wife as per the conditions laid down by the patriarchal society.

Phoolwati from the same novel is also presented as an unprototypical image of woman. She used to live in a village, while her husband, Shambhu ran a tea stall in the city and carried on an affair with Magoo. After he is murdered by Magoo's husband, his death does not evoke the traditional wails of grief and helplessness from Phoolwati but she rejoices in his death, as she did not like his behaviour. She also feels like rewarding the murderer for punishing Shambhu for his act. The norm of wife being beaten by her husband is inverted in case of her relationship as she kicks Shambhu on one occasion when he got drunk and tried to bully her. She is not cowed down by the bullying Sundar Pahalwan, and courageously faces him. This makes him admire her. He marries her but the marriage does not present picture of male oppression of the female. Before accepting the marriage proposal she puts down three conditions for marriage. As Gudiya tells us: "Sundar Pahalwan had proposed marriage to Phoolwati. She agreed, but her assent was subject to certain conditions. These were, firstly that he would build a pucca house for her, the ownership of which would be irrevocably hers, secondly, that he would allow her to continue running her businesses as before and, thirdly, that Sundar Pahalwan was to treat me as their adoptive daughter." (179)

Phoolwati's acceptance of marriage proposal based on the conditions is again against the established norms of patriarchal set-up whereby the boy demands or puts conditions and the girl or her parents have to accept them. Here the bride thinks about her future security. Phoolwati's practicality and her unsentimental nature are at complete variance with the traditional picture of woman in Indian society. These qualities save her from disintegrating after Sundar Pahalwan is murdered. No doubt, she feels grief-stricken and subdued and suffers from occasional bouts of sadness.

Shakuntala in *Shakuntala: The Play of Memory* stayed with her widowed mother in a mountain country. After the death of her father, who was a vaidya, her mother carried on with his profession. Shakuntala was restless to see the world, to wander with the freedom of birds and clouds. Sita in Anita Desai's *Where Shall We Go This Summer?* also has the desire to be free and is discontented with a woman's life. Shakuntala is married to Srijan. For her, marriage is an escape from the existing conditions in her mother's house where she could not seek freedom:

> I knew there was more inside me than the limits of my experience dictated. I thirsted for glimpses of new lands, people, ideas. It was as if the move from my mother's home to my husband's—the half-a-day journey from one village to another—had suddenly made the impossible possible. A man's equal in bed, why could I not desire what men enjoyed: the freedom to wander, to be elsewhere, to seek, and perhaps find . . . something? (48)

Stifled by social custom, hungry for experience, she deserts home and family for the company of a Greek horse merchant, whom she meets by the river Ganga. Together they travel far and wide and surrender to unbridled pleasure, as Shakuntala assumes the identity of Yaduri, the fallen woman. Here again Shakuntala is shown to have broken the convention whereby traditionally an Indian married woman is expected to be loyal and faithful to her husband till her death. But Shakuntala in her quest for experience and knowledge breaks the traditional norms. Here the novelist seems to suggest that if a woman desires, she can choose her own path. The instances cited from the novels of Gokhale and other novelists indicate that women are not afraid of violating the traditional code of conduct when occasion demands.

Women characters in Namita Gokhale's novels show exemplary courage and strength in the times of crisis. Ammi, Phoolwati, Gudiya and Rachita struggle hard and never think of defeat at the hands of men. They neither give up their efforts nor do they give in. Instead of being emotional they come out to be practical and pragmatic. The matter of providing financial security no longer remains the privilege of men.

In *Paro: Dreams of Passion*, Paro, who belongs to a middle-class family, gets married to the business tycoon, B.R. After their divorce she uses his money for survival. How the man-made laws of the society of which she is part are to be exploited she is fully aware of. When Priya questions Paro regarding using B.R.'s money and how she survived, her curt reply is:

> "Stock, shares, family property—the occasional sale of some jewellery," she replied airily. "And, of course, Babu settled some property on me after our marriage. The rent is enough for my simple needs."
>
> "But is that right? I mean, you left him, don't you feel funny using his money?" I would persist.
>
> "Look, sweetie," she would say, her eyes darkening, "they made the rules." (34)

Later on she gets into relationship with a number of people who were rich like 'Bucky' Bhandpur, Lenin, Shambhu Nath Mishra, the congress politician and Loukas Leoros, the European film director. She even went to America for a World Conference along with Shambhu Nath Mishra. Paro used the money of the people she came in contact with, to meet her expenses and live life lavishly.

Priya worked as the secretary of B.R., the owner of Sita Sewing Machines, before her marriage. After her marriage with Suresh for some time she does not work but later she takes up a part-time job in her friend's small bookshop in the Oberoi Hotel to escape from her empty home as Suresh was too busy with his cases. He was quite apprehensive about her taking up the job. His reaction was one of a typical husband. He urged Priya to think about his position in the society and about people's comments. But Priya was unmoved as she narrates: "But I was unmoved for that job represented escape from my empty home. Of course, it wasn't my first job either, for I had put in three years of service with Sita Sewing Machines. It was pleasant to earn some money again however little it might be." (100)

In Gokhale's *Gods, Graves and Grandmother* the women are projected as self-dependent and she empowers them to face the harsh social reality. These women are not cowed down by the adversities. They do not brood over their misfortunes or indulge in self-pity but face the world bravely and become financially well-settled. Subhash Chandra observes: "They eminently succeed in carving a niche for themselves in the male-dominated society, and prove to themselves and others that woman is equal to man when it comes to crisis-management and survival in the face of destructive social forces. They turn themselves into subjects, performing acts and desiring men and things. They prove themselves to be achievers in the face of odds society necessarily places in the way of women. Rather than conform to some definition of woman by the social system, these women succeed in defining themselves."[13]

Gudiya and her grandmother, after they are thrown out of their haveli, have to take shelter in a Delhi lane where they build a jhuggi. Grandmother is not deterred by the difficulties she faces. She builds up a small make-shift temple using the things available at hand. She steals the marble slab from the building site behind her jhuggi, places it beneath the peepal tree which shaded hut and finds five rounded river stones from sahib's rockery and arranges them on marble slab. She gets marigold flowers from sahib's garden and a stainless steel thali which belonged to her daughter to complete the shrine. Even though they are Muslims, the old woman acts as the Pujarin of the temple, collecting the proceeds from the offerings made by the devotees. As Ammi belonged to family of singing prostitutes, she utilizes her art for singing bhajans, thus enthralling the audience and turning them into committed devotees. Such devotees do not hesitate to make offerings.

Janaki Venkataraman analyses Ammi's sense of utilizing the available resources: "Ammi, who knows only too well that in certain social situations, religion is merely a convenient disguise to wear, begins her saintly career with a piece of purloined marble, rocks stolen from a neighbourhood rockery, and a firm faith in her own ability to belt out soul-stirring bhajans. Her ascendance to mystic status, and relative financial security is swift and unstoppable."[14]

The temple continues to prosper, and expand as the generous offerings multiply manifold. Gudiya narrates the growing prosperity of the temple: "Money poured in eight annas, five rupee coins, even the occasional fifty rupee note. The miracles were not yet manifest, but we were already rich beyond wildest dreams. We had no neighbours to discredit us, and as the tea-shop wallah also shared in our sudden prosperity, having diversified into the sale of coconuts and marigold garlands, we faced no scepticism from that quarter." (4)

Apart from Ammi and Gudiya, other people like Phoolwati, Pandit Kailash Shastry, beggars etc., who come in contact with the temple, also flourished. Phoolwati who comes from a small place in district Madhubani, Bihar, settles well in metropolitan city like Delhi. She takes charge of her husband's business courageously. She possessed a better head for business than her husband. She was much focused and her business acumen could be seen when she negotiated a reduced five-year rental from the street lord Sundar Pahalwan, with a percentage of the take thrown in.

Phoolwati also diversifies her business to increase her earnings and sets up a stall just outside the temple which sold incense, marigold garlands, coconuts and little brass amulets. She also gets Ammi's coloured photograph in the form of postcard printed and sells them on her stall. She fully knows how to get benefitted in any situation. She becomes financially independent and has good entrepreneurial skills. She also looks after the financial matters of the temple.

Another character from the novel, Roxanne Lamba, is also financially independent. She is the Principal of St. Jude's Academy for the Socially Handicapped where Gudiya studies. She is portrayed stronger than her husband, with lofty ideals, committed to the cause of education for the deprived children, while Mr. Lamba is an appendage, has no profession, no ideals, no commitment except to enjoy life on his rich wife's resources. All these women characters show exemplary courage and strength in the times of crisis which is similar to Shobha De's women characters. In her novels women characters like Aasha Rani, Karuna, Mikky and Amrita struggle for survival and never think of defeat at the hands of men. Rachita Tiwari in *The Book of Shadows* is also financially independent. She is a lecturer teaching English literature in Jesus and Mary College, New Delhi.

Some of the women characters exibit self-reliance in financial matters. They use their abilities, courage and shrewdness not only to stand on their own legs but also to prosper by leaps and bounds.

Women characters in Namita Gokhale's novels have met with different experiences in their struggle towards emancipation, empowerment and search for self-identity. Some of them meet tragic death or rejoin their husbands or get ready to face the world alone without the support of men in their lives. Paro, who has successfully handled all her amorous adventures and who is thought to be the spokesperson or 'the free woman, symbol and prototype of emancipation and individuality,' (48) realizes that without her beauty and physical charm she cannot impress and control men.

Over a period of time she has relationship with various men belonging to varied professions and interest. To assert her beauty she even establishes relationship with the ugliest person like Shambhu Nath Mishra. This relationship puzzles Priya and when she questions Paro, she honestly replies that he is ugly and he makes her feel beautiful. Therefore, at the end of novel, she throws a party to celebrate her recovery from a near fatal accident and in the party she slashes her wrist and dies. Thus, she brings an end to her meaningless sex-adventure spree.

Priya also imitates Paro to some extent. Through Priya's diary, Suresh finds out about the relationship she had with B.R. He is shocked and hurt and tells Priya that for some time they should live apart to think over matters. Priya goes to Bombay to her brother. On reaching Bombay, she felt lonely in the vastness of the city. She stayed with her brother's family but later on shifted to her mother's flat. There also she feels lonely and the present and past ghosts haunt her. To pass the time she re-reads Rebecca and feels betrayed: "Once again I abandoned myself to the fantasies of my youth. Only rereading it now, I felt betrayed, utterly betrayed. Rebecca had after all, done nothing wrong; the dazzlers in the new pulp paperbacks committed adultery almost as a rite of passage. Rebecca's only fault was that she was strong, stronger than Max! Not very profound observation, I am sure but for me they held the blinding flash of revelation. My entire system of values was suddenly upturned I felt a spiteful anger for that lying dog-eared novel, and wanted above all to tear it to smithereens and consign it to the dark monsoon sea." (137)

The painful realization, 'I am an Indian woman and for me my husband is my God' (137) dawned upon her. She dreamt of Suresh during her troubled intermittent sleep and wrote letters asking for his forgiveness. When he did not respond, she tried to commit suicide by going into the sea but the sharp bite of a jellyfish turned her back towards the sea-shore. She then reached B.R.'s house and her love for him overtook her for a while. After a brief telephonic talk with Suresh, Priya felt a sudden surge of joy. She returned home acutely aware of her roots as she herself confessed that being an Indian woman her husband was her god.

Ammi in *Gods, Graves and Grandmother*, after her struggle for self-assertion, manages to obtain not only respectability but a sort of 'sainthood' with a considerable number of followers. Even a memorial with her marble statue was dedicated to her. Gudiya realizes after a few months of an unhappy married life, that she cannot waste her life with a person like Kalki. She was expecting Kalki's child conceived before their marriage but his behaviour towards her was callous and indifferent. Phoolwati advises her to consider her husband Kalki 'a disposable being' and tells her that she cannot waste her entire life with those bandwallahs. Gudiya makes up her mind. She sells her jewellery and gets a ticket for Bombay for Kalki and sends him to Bombay to try his luck in films. She misses Kalki at times, but takes his absence as an opportunity for growth, for escape. As she asserts: "I missed him, but I sensed in his absence an opportunity for growth, for escape, which I was determined not to miss. I loved Kalki, but love is not life, and the imperatives of survival pulled elsewhere. Every day, gradually and imperceptibly, his hold on me lessened." (224-25)

After Kalki's departure, she gives birth to his daughter and starts living with Phoolwati. She looks to her future life with optimism. She says: "When enough time passes and the dust settles on those troubled memories, perhaps I shall be able to embellish them with a veil of fabulism and mystery. Rendering the past acceptable, if not accountable, is a talent I inherited from my Ammi. It is easy to live in the present." (239-40)

After Sundar Pahalwan is murdered, Phoolwati does not become a helpless wreck. She remains in control of her business and her life, exhibiting in no way that she cannot do without male support. However, she is unhappy to lose her second husband, Sundar whom she had come to love for his qualities. Whenever she remembers Sundar, she cries. But she has the capacity to carry on with life and face the situation boldly and hence she spends her life with Gudiya and her daughter, Mallika.

Parvati in *A Himalayan Love Story,* becomes mad after the death of Lalit, her husband and birth of her daughter. She is kept in asylum in Bareilly. Later on she is left in the care of her daughter Irra. Rachita in *The Book of Shadows*, learns her lessons from nature and a chance encounter with the mirror brings the confidence back in her. Without any improvement in her outward appearance, she comes to terms with life as a constant process of making and re-making oneself: "To be ourselves we must remain in control of our scripts. We must make and remake ourselves, possess and repossess our world, cast and recast our lot in every precious moment. Above all, we must know what to hold on to, what to discard, in this radical flux which is life. "I felt disquietingly alive. My repertoire of memory had run out; I had bid farewell to the world of my confabulations. I had acquired, achieved, possessed myself again." (229)

Rachita does not know whether she will return to the world she had left behind or not. But she is optimistic that even if other things perish, the hillside, the snow-mountains will remain. Nature will carry on with its activities and so will Rachita carry on with her life: "This hillside will remain as will the snow mountains that watch over us, even if nothing else does. The garden will bloom again, the roses by the veranda, the weeds and forget-me-nots by the gravel path. I think I know that I will remain." (232)

Shakuntala in *Shakuntala: The Play of Memory* in pursuit of knowledge and experience reaches Kashi, the city of her imagination, along with the Greek traveller. But later she is filled with remorse and longs to return to Srijan, her husband and her home. She cannot return now and she blames herself: "It is the nature of night to follow day, and day to follow night. It is the nature of water to flow. It is the nature of women to have children and grandchildren and see them grow. There is a child in my belly and I have fled from our home. What madness overcame me that day by the river. Perhaps that woman Kamalini, my dimly remembered rival, had cast a spell upon me. Perhaps it was not her doing at all, for I was born under the star of exile, like my namesake Shakuntala." (166)

Shakuntala becomes restless. She realizes that the time has come to leave Nearchus although she loves him. She leaves the house at dawn and goes to Kashi, her destination. There she thinks of going to a monastery, a Buddhist Sangha as she thinks that they might show some consideration for a woman like her. She can become a Sakya nun like Srijan's mother. Engrossed in her thoughts, Shakuntala strayed into the middle of a lane only to be attacked by the bull. The bull buried its horns in her stomach. Wounded Shakuntala, with a torn womb without her baby, is carried by the Buddhist nun to her dwelling where she nurses Shakuntala and repeatedly tells her to embrace the Buddha. But Shakuntala would not bow to her wishes. She realizes that death is approaching near. She gives a brave fight but ultimately dies with determination to return again to the earth: "As a flame is extinguished so I had died in Kashi, which was a blessing. But I did not will it so. The bile, the defeat, the ignominy in this death—I rejected it. I would not depart humiliated from these shores. I would hide, escape, return to the earth and the rocks that knew me, and the parrots, and the patient fisherman who sat by the banks of the Ganga, baiting her fish." (198)

Thus, we find that Namita Gokhale in her novels has portrayed the emerging new empowered woman. No doubt Paro, Priya, Ammi, Gudiya, Phoolwati, Parvati, Rachita and Shakuntala face problems and difficulties but they have tried to overcome them and get themselves empowered to some extent without male support. Through her novels she has deconstructed the very concept of femininity which aimed at women to be docile, submissive, chaste and modest. Her characters face unfavourable circumstances but they struggle and assert themselves.

Paro in *Paro: Dreams of Passion* was forced by the circumstances to exploit her own sexuality for self-identity and self-assertion. She has succeeded to some extent in coming out of the stereotype image of women where they were believed to be biologically unfit to assume responsibility and hence needed male protection and guidance. But ultimately she was tired of the life she had chosen and succumbs under the impact of factors beyond her control.

Priya from the same novel, on the other hand, tried to rise above her middle-class background by imitating Paro. She sought empowerment through sexual autonomy by having relationship with B.R. and getting married to Suresh on the basis of his financial status.

Ammi in *Gods, Graves and Grandmother* started a new life in the slums and was able to give an 'aura' to her past life and died a 'saint' in the eyes of her followers. Gudiya desired Kalki against the convention, got married to him, helped him to go to Bombay and forgot him in due course of time. She was practical enough to start living in the present with the support of Phoolwati and her daughter. Phoolwati was also empowered. She struggled against all odds and successfully ran her husband's business, remarried Sundar Pahalwan and continued with her life after his death. All the three women in the novel are endowed with well-defined identities, possess stronger personalities and have tremendous innate resources to grapple with the crisis life is vulnerable to.

Parvati in *A Himalayan Love Story* seeks emancipation through sexual autonomy but as prophesied becomes mad. Rachita in *The Book of Shadows* fights her own battle after the acid attack. Nature helps her sustain life when she comes to live in Himalayan retreat of Ranikhet. Shakuntala in *Shakuntala: The Play of Memory* desires to live on her own terms but it is thwarted at every turn by circumstances and the age in which she lives. Her attempt for empowerment meets a tragic end.

Namita Gokhale has pointed out that the aim of the tradition of feminism whether Western or Eastern is to improve the lot of women in every field of life. She realistically brought out the problems women normally face. In her novels, some women have failed while others succeeded in their endeavour to overcome obstacles. These characters whether successful or not, attempt to assert themselves even when fortune refuses to smile on them. In their attempts at self-assertion, some women have no grudge in violating the established code of conduct. Some confident and courageous characters refuse to rely on men for financial needs. They use their abilities and acumen to attain financial independence.

NOTES

1. Sushila Singh, "Preface," *Feminism and Recent Fiction in English*. New Delhi: Prestige, 1991, p. 7

2. N. Krishnaswamy, et.al, qtd. *Contemporary Literary Theory*. New Delhi: MacMillan, 2001, p. 73.
3. John Singleton, "The Writing Self," *The Creative Writing Workbook*. New York: Palgrave, 2001, p. 23.
4. Linda Gordon, Qtd., "Preface," Sushila Singh, *Feminism and Recent Fiction in English*, p. 115.
5. Simone de Beauvoir, *The Second Sex*, trans. and ed. H.M. Parshley, London: Jonathan Capé, 1953, rpt. Harmondsworth: Penguin, 1983, p. 16.
6. Betty Friedan, *The Feminine Mystique*. 1963, rpt. Harmondsworth: Penguin, 1971, p. 282.
7. Alladi Uma, "Women and Her Family," *Indian and Afro-Amercian—A Literary Perspective*. New Delhi: Sterling, 1989, p. 4.
8. Kuldeep Kumar and Gajendra Kumar. "Deconstructing Femininity: A Reading of Namita Gokhale's *Paro: Dreams of Passion*," *Indian English Literature*, ed. Basavraj Naikar, New Delhi: Atlantic, 2002, Vol. I, p. 153.
9. Veena Singh, "Woman as Portrayed by the Women Novelists of India," *The Brown Critique*, No. 10-12, Oct-Dec 1995, p. 36.
10. Nilufer Ferheiz C. Bharucha, "Namita Gokhale's *Paro: Dreams of Passion:* Meaning through Mediocrity" *Indian Woman Novelists*, ed. R.K. Dhawan, Set II, Vol VI, New Delhi: Prestige, 1993. p. 68.
11. P. Ramamoorthy, "My Life is my Own: A Study of Shashi Deshpande's Women," Feminism and Recent Fiction in English, ed. Sushila Singh, p. 115.
12. Subhash Chandra, "The New Woman in Namita Gokhale's Gods, Graves and Grandmother," Indian Women Novelists, Set III, Vol. 6. ed. R.K. Dhawan, p. 18.
13. Subhash Chandra, "Female Subjectivity and Female Empowerment in the Fiction of Namita Gokhale," *The Literary Voice,* No. 3, February 1996, p. 55.
14. Janaki Venkataraman, "Arrested Flight," *Indian Review of Books*, 16 Dec. 1994-15 Jan. 1995, p. 33.

Romantic Recollections

Whatever is strange, beautiful, remote and unfamiliar is romantic. Namita Gokhale has nostalgic memories of the past. Though born in Lucknow, she spent her early childhood in Nainital. For her, Nainital is not a place on a map, it is not even a geographical location but it exists continually for her wherever she goes. The moment she visits the places of past, all the recollections crowd in the mind. As she admits: "The overlays of remembrance and memory had coalesced into a dream territory which some part of me continued to inhabit."[1]

These remembrances give her an inspiration to describe the places, persons and sites she encountered in the past. Her memory is crowded with even the smaller things: "These were memories made up of brittle things: the texture of sticky summer lychees; the sound of langurs tramping about on the tin roof; the taste of fresh pine and deodar needles which the mali's son insisted tasted 'just like chewing gum.' And our Malju, the mali, the wizard, who fell off tiffin top chasing an errant cow."[2]

Her love for the Himalayas and Nainital is reflected in her novels. Places assume importance in the works of writers. Many instances can be cited to show that old places are re-created. Thomas Hardy refers to Wessex and William Wordsworth to Lake District. Jayant Mahapatra and A.K. Ramanujan reveal their relation with their region. Namita Gokhale has fond memories of the places she lived in or was associated with. These recollections are reflected when she describes the places in her novels.

In *Paro: Dreams of Passion* we have graphic description of the places. In the beginning of the novel, Priya describes B.R.'s office, where she was employed. All the girls working in the office had crush on B.R. and served him devotedly. They thought his office to be a temple and his room, the sanctum sanctorum. Priya tells us: "B.R. had decorated the office himself. It was like the temple of Pallas Athene for us. The dear white lines of formica, the immaculate swivel chairs, the perfectly tended potted plants, as perfectly tended as the oyster-pale nails of his personal secretary." (1)

Namita Gokhale is a keen observer and her description some times has a touch of humour. Priya's house has been described by her without missing the minutest details. She even tells us the exact dimensions of the room: "The room was still the same fifteen feet by twenty; it still housed the same divan-cum-bed at one end, and the same precarious table with the four even more precarious dining chairs at the other. The glum framed photograph of my deceased father was also garlanded. The radio with its crocheted cover and crown of plastic flowers was, as ever, turned to Radio Ceylon, but the pale of depression that normally crept like gloam-dust into our house was absent." (18-19) It is a typical middle-class household of Mumbai where there is a constraint of space. The single room was utilized as living room, dinning room, bedroom and a place to worship god.

Namita Gokhale has witnessed death from close quarters, as her husband, mother-in-law and sister-in-law died in front of her eyes. She herself had a close brush with death. Hence in her novels, she has written about death quite often. As Quiser Zoha Alam observes: "In Victorian literature sex was often a taboo but death was talked about again and again whereas in modern literature death is generally a taboo but they take up sex freely."[3]

Gokhale has, however, discussed and described death and death scenes several times in her novels. In *Paro: Dreams of Passion*, she has described the cremation ground. Lenin and

Priya visit the ghat after Paro has been cremated: "We entered through somewhat ornate gates. There were bodies burning in neat little rows right from the entrance. No one seemed to be around. Some of the fires were burning high and bright, others were almost extinguished." (170)

In *Gods, Graves and Grandmother*, Namita Gokhale has described the places in Delhi. Gudiya describes the street outside the kotha of her grandmother: "Carriages, buggies, Rolls Royces and Daimlers used to line up outside the house in the evening. Perfume from the flowering mogra and chameli spilled out into the street, and if a man were to innocently walk past that house, when he got home his wife or mistress would sniff suspiciously and ask where he had been." (5)

The account gives one an idea about the flourishing business of the kotha. Then the writer describes the street of Delhi when Gudiya lost her way home. On one side of the road there were office buildings and on the other there were the pavement dwellers who were busy in their daily activities: "The complexion of the area changed and I found myself on a street with a lot of office buildings. Groups of families—pavement dwellers—were herded around merry little fires of newspaper, packing cases and twigs. The delicious aroma of cooking arose from shining brass pots bubbling atop makeshift three-brick ovens. Old women were telling bedtime stories to their children." (113-14)

Namita Gokhale spent her early childhood in Nainital. She has nostalgic memories of Nainital. She is quite familiar with the topography, climate, people, rituals and even the myths associated with various places there. All these recollections are expressed in her novel. *A Himalayan Love Story*, whose setting is in Nainital for most of the part of the novel. For Gokhale, Nainital is part of her being. As she herself admits: "For me, Nainital is not a place on a map, it is not even a geographical location. It exists continually for me wherever I go. I live out a part of my life there wherever else in the world I might be."[4]

In *A Himalayan Love Story* we have apt description of the places in Nainital and also the Jeolikote situated in the Himalayas, on the road leading to Nainital. The houses, roads, bazars etc. are described in details in the novel. In the beginning of the novel there is the description of life in Jeolikote where Parvati lived along with her mother in two rooms perched above a kirana shop. Parvati tells about various trades undertaken by the hill people living there. The people traded on the things which were available in the hills and earned money for their livelihood: "Strawberries, mulberries and roasted corn on the cob were the staples of trade in Jeolikote, apart, of course, from the honey for which it was justly famous. It was not a prosperous town, nor a particularly interesting one. Subjects of conversation were few and far between; nothing much happened except for yet another tourist or traveller taking sick because of the winding roads and pucking uninhibitedly out of the window onto the body of a bus." (4)

Then we have the description of the road in Nainital which led to the place where Nandashtami mela was held every year. Namita Gokhale has furnished minutest details reflecting her close love for Nainital and things associated with it .Mukul, along with Jeevan Jaundice and Mohan Mischief went to the mela. He describes the road leading to the mela: "We walked past the old English graveyard of St. Johns-in-the-Wilderness, with its brooding trees, with roots like talons, past the stable where houses sheltered restlessly under tattered blankets, down past the mosque and the police station to the temple." (HLS, 83)

Further he describes the mela: "The comforting glow of lights from the temple decorations came into view. Rows upon rows of coloured bulbs were strung radially into an incandescent tent. Even the gurdwara was gaily illuminated. Many of the shops were already half shut. Their owners lay dozing inside.

Shawls and bangles and ribbons were hung in confused colourful display. Sticky looking jalebis and other sweetmeats were piled in unappetizing heaps beside enormous frying pots." (84)

Gokhale's fascination for hills is again evident in her next novel, *The Book of Shadows*, which is set in the Himalayan retreat of Ranikhet. It was a place developed by the Britishers as a hill station, a place of retreat and rest for their soldiers, an alternative from the intense heat of the plains. When William James Cockerell, a missionary arrived at Ranikhet to begin his mission along with his wife it was scarcely populated. There was not a single house at the site. The place was covered with trees. William Cockerell describes: "With the exception of a little land cleared on one side, the country around was covered with forests of pine, oak and rhododendron, interspersed with meadows or 'bugyals' where the people of the valleys pastured their cattle." (37)

Rachita Tiwari had sought refuge in a remote house in the Himalayan foothills, after the attack by her former lover's sister. This was the house which she used to frequent as a child. Namita Gokhale, in the Author's note written in the beginning of the book, writes that she has lived in the house mentioned in the novel. So also commenting upon the house she says: "My husband and I lived in an old house in the hills. It was a house we both fell in love with. But we also felt that there was something strange some presence that was not entirely at peace with itself. I based my novel on that house. I didn't set out to do it. I didn't say, 'Okay, I've been to a haunted house so I'm going to write a ghost story.' It happened rather insidiously."[5]

The house in the novel was built by an English missionary, William James Cockerell in 1868. The superstitious locals felt that it was situated on an inauspicious spot. It witnessed a sequence of owners, each more bizarre than the last. The English missionary, who met an untimely death, was followed by Captain Walter Wolcott of the English Army. Somewhat of an aesthete he lived there with Dona Rosa a clairvoyant wandering through India. Wolcott was burnt due to fire, this made the English Army take over the house with Osborne, the Colonel Regiment being the next owner. Munro and Marcus also lived in the house. After their death Father Benedictus, a Catholic priest lived in the house befriending the spirit which lived behind the curtain. Father Benedictus perishes while trying to exorcise the ghosts of the dead Munro and Marcus from the house leaving it to be occupied by Rachita. She writes about the house with the old outhouse where she played as a child: "There it stood, in all its loveliness. A gracious veranda encircled its contours. The white blooms of climbing roses clung to the frontage. The windows of the upstairs bedrooms gazed out at the sweep of the Himalayan ranges, now obscured from view. Broken stone steps led down from the garden to the tennis court below, or to what had once been the tennis court but was now an overgrowth of bramble and nettle. The garden was covered with dandelion and forget-me-not, although some clumps of lupin and larkspur struggled against the chaos of weed. The two hydrangea bushes were where they had always been; they had grown to monstrous proportions, the blue flowers streaked and spotted with purple." (9-10)

The house was mysterious and so also were its surroundings. Rachita once went for a walk on the road that unfolded in the hill below the house. Rachita found a spot on the road which was mysterious with a little water fall. On seeing the beauty of the place, she forgot about herself and her struggle for search of identity. The spot had a soothing effect on Rachita which makes her forget herself. She describes the beauty of the place: "There is a path that unfolds in the hills below the house, that winds around until you reach the stream beside the fields, and then back to the house again. There is a spot in that walk that I have always felt is enchanted, privy to secrets, peopled by sprites or fairies or some such benevolent spirits. A copse of banj, of

Himalayan oak, is clustered around a little waterfall that tumbles prettily to a clear pool surrounded by a heap of dolmen-like rocks. There was a forest of ferns around me, delicate cautious tendrils of the most heart-rending green. I sat down on a rock and contemplated the scene, forgetting for a white the confusing dilemmas of identity." (69)

Another place that had an impact on Rachita was the Bhairav Temple. It terrified her even as a child. It was a forbidden place where even sun never paid a visit. It was dedicated to the fiercest of hill deity. Rachita again on one of her walks reached the temple and on reaching there shuddered with fear. She narrates her observations: "I found myself on the rocky path that leads to the Bhairav mandir dedicated to the fiercest of our hill deities. The temple is a forbidding place. It is situated upon a curve of the hill which the sun never visits. A jagged assembly of boulders line the way to the temple gates. A concatenation of crows is always squabbling there. Several steps up, on the spine of a ridge that straddles the montainscape, in a direction o obverse to the lay of the land, the Bhairav temple used to terrify me even as a child. Now, once again, the hair on my arms stood on edge as I walked up the sombre path." (197)

Gokhale's love for the hills continues even in her next novel, *Shakuntala: The Play of Memory*. Shakuntala, the protagonist, lived in the hills of north India, just like Shakuntala of Kalidasa's epic. The life of the people of the hills was difficult with very few basic amenities and comforts. For even the basic need of water, they had to travel long distance down the hill. Their huts were damp and many small creatures inhabited the place along with the humans. Shakuntala would often wake up at night with a spider or a centipede on the straw bed on which she slept: "I grew up in the mountain country, like the Shakuntala of the epic. The hill people from our parts were called vanvasis, dwellers of the forests. It was a harsh life, of very few comforts, and our ways were far removed from those of the nagariks or city folk.

We had little water to wash, for it was carried up from a great distance down the hill. Yet our house was always cold, or damp, or wet, as was the firewood, which burned badly and ruined our eyes. I often woke up with a hairy spider or an adventurous centipede sharing the pallet of lumpy straw on which I slept." (8)

Shakuntala had a desire to see the unseen and know the unknown. Hence she keenly observes the things around her. When she ran away with the Greek horse merchant in pursuit of her desire, he took her to summer festival. As a part of festivities, Kalidasa's drama, Shakuntala was performed. Shakuntala gives the details about the place and arrangements made for the drama: "We arrived at a magnificent pleasure garden. An elaborate pavilion stood at one end, decorated with streamers and toranas of tender mango leaves. The grass was freshly watered, and the summer dust had thankfully settled. Our hosts—for there were more than one, Nearchus's friend having joined with others in his guild to prepare the festivities—greeted us with garlands. Marble benches were placed among the flowers and bushes, and woven straw mats laid out for those nagariks who wished to seat themselves on the ground. Lotus-leaf fans were distributed to the guests. A panoplied stage had been set up in the pavilion, and we were informed that a play, the greatest drama ever written, was being enacted as part of the celebrations." (145)

After leaving Nearchus, Shakuntala goes to Kashi on the other side of the river Ganga, the Kashi of her yearning, where she had not yet gone. As she climbs the steps towards Kashi, she witnesses men and women busy in their own activity. Shakuntala narrates: "Well, I could not sit there forever, and in a while I started climbing up the steps. I was out of breath, and for the first time I could feel the weight of the baby I carried. Other people were appearing in the ghats now, men and women and children, more people than I had ever seen. As I walked along the upper edge of the steps I realised that the river was as full of activity as the city was. It was an extension of Kashi, or perhaps even the other way around, the city flowing around the river in varying eddies, currents and pool of stillness. Holy men with matted locks stood single—legged in the crane-mudra, offering oblations to the morning sun. Women of all ages were gathering water in brass urns. Crows and sparrows pecked at rice and grain lay scattered as offerings." (181-82)

A large number of Gokhale's characters come alive before our eyes because of the faithful depiction of their physical appearance. Namita Gokhale has drawn characters from amongst the people she encountered in her life. She has a very minute observation and unerringly caught the apparently trivial and small gestures which gave a character his individuality. This enables us to grasp it firmly.

In *Paro: Dreams of Passion* Priya, the observant narrator closely watches every move of Paro. She describes the physical appearance of Paro and the activities she undertook very minutely. Priya saw herself in Paro and therefore closely monitored her presence. In the beginning of the novel we are told about the bridal attire of Paro: "She was wearing a silver tissue sari, and was positively glittering with diamonds. They were strewn like dewdrops over her chokers, pendants, rings, bangles, sequins. Tall as she was, she was balancing on the highest stiletto heels I had ever seen in my life. Even her payals were encrusted with incredibly real-looking diamonds. Her lipstick was a pale silver, and silver eye-shadow gleamed over her hard eyes." (10)

After the marriage to B.R., Paro would pay visits to his office and would not answer or acknowledge the greetings of the staff members. She would come with loads of expensive shopping with everything matching in her attire, from saree to sandals and flowers tucked in her hair. Paro was fond of dressing up. Priya describes the attire of Paro worn for the chic cocktail party hosted by Lenin's industrialist friend at his farmhouse:

"She dressed to the hilt, in a full green-and-gold South Indian silk which reflected the colour of her eyes, somehow. She wore a lot of old-fashioned jewellery as well, and flowers in her hair." (63)

The description of Shambhu Nath Mishra, the controversial politician belonging to congress party seems very apt and displays Gokhale's fine sense of observation tinged with humour. The enigma of the disproportionate power emanated from his strange personality. Paro was mesmerized by him and their affair became one of the hottest scandals of the year. According to Priya he was the ugliest, grossest and vilest man, she had ever encountered. She describes him: "He was black as the night, black as the carpet, and his belly protruded obscenely from his chest, like a fat rotting pear. All this was balanced on the thinnest, spindliest legs possible. An immaculately starched white khadi topi nestled on his thick, suspiciously black hair." (79)

Namita Gokhale here has used figurative language to bring out the character of Shambhu Nath Mishra. Then we have the description of Paro's friend Lenin, who was the son of the Minister of State for Industry. Lenin's actual name was Avinendra but due to his Marxist leanings Priya called him Lenin. M.E. Derret remarks regarding the characterization in the Indo-Anglian novel, "A character who may appear to us to be a highly individual and masterly creation may quite easily have been drawn from real live."[7] Namita Gokhale also had a cousin called Lenin and her uncle was called Stalin.

Priya tells about Lenin that he was studying for his Ph.D. and at the same time was also writing a book. He was absolutely besotted by Paro, to the utter shock of his parents. For Priya, Lenin looked so young that Paro appeared to be his mother. Priya writes: "He looked young enough to be her son. He was a thin youth in a white kurta-pyjama, with a straggly beard, and an ethereal look, and looked a sort of oriental Jesus Christ with a faintly obese Mary Magdalen." (43)

That Namita Gokhale chose for her novels the characters from amongst the people around her is again evident in her next novel *Gods, Graves and Grandmother*. Residing in Delhi she is fully aware of the life in Delhi high society as well as the slums which have now become part and parcel of the city life. In the novel the slum life with its multifarious activities is depicted. As the temple flourishes so also the people who have attached themselves to it also prosper. Amongst them was Pandit Kailash Shastry, a man with a felicity for words which made his speech charming to the listeners. Gudiya gives the details: "The Brahmin was a thin, meek looking man. His starched white dhoti spread out in an exquisite fan to reveal surprisingly muscular calves. He wore thick eyeglasses and an air of supplication. In spite of his deceptively insignificant looks, when he talked, the very air sat still and the crows came out of their rookeries to listen." (59)

Then Gudiya gives description of Kalki, whom she married later on. He was handsome with princely profile which attracted Gudiya. His handsome profile could make any girl fall in love with him irrespective of his family background, financial and social status: "He was so handsome that I could feel my insides quiver. He had a perfectly proportioned nose and a noble profile. He looked like a Rajput prince. He was shabbily dressed and his polished leather shoes had gaping holes through which I could see his torn socks and dirty feet." (111)

Gudiya was so impressed by Kalki's looks that she instantly fell in love with him and did not bother even to find out his family background. Gudiya was also impressed by Malvika Mehta, the new teacher in her school. She had done her graduation from the Delhi School of Social Work and ran a counselling programme for underprivileged students. She represented everything Gudiya wanted to be. This yearning is typical of any girl of her age residing in slums. Gudiya minutely describes her: "She was extremely good looking. She had creamy white skin, jet-black hair, cut in a short, extremely fashionable style, and a lascivious mole poised over her succulent lips. She was dressed in simple clothes that I suspected of being very expensive." (124)

A Himalayan Love Story, Gokhale's next novel is also replete with descriptions of people. The people here belong to the hills, unlike the people in previous novels who came from urban areas. In the beginning we have the description of Hiranand Joshi, Parvati's uncle. Hiranand Joshi was the step-brother of Parvati's mother. He was an educated man and was the principal of Manava Public School in Nainital. He lived in an odd looking cottage called Wee Nooke. Parvati tells: "Masterji was several years older than my mother. He had never married. It was rumoured that he had taken a vow of chastity after reading the collected works of Swami Vivekananda. He was a thin, stern man with a kind smile. I found his habitual silence reassuring and he seemed relieved by my lack of conversation." (21-22)

Then we have the graphic description of the Tibetan woman selling tiny scent bottles and heavily-set stone jewellery. To Gokhale this scene was not unfamiliar. The Tibetans are to be found everywhere in India selling their goods. Mukul goes on to describe the Tibetan woman towards whom he was attracted for a while. He tells us: "A young Tibetan woman was sitting alone at a stall near the temple, quite indifferent to her surroundings. Dressed in a long black baku, she was half reclining upon a battered tin trunk, her wares spread out on the ground before her. Her slanting Mongolian eyes were heavily made up, their clear almond shape emphasized by the thick eyeliner." (84-85)

In the novel we also have the description of the mother of Jeewan Jaundice, Sohan Selfish and Mohan Mischief, Ija. Mukul, after looking at her thought that, she was the oldest woman he had seen for a long time. She displayed all the signs of her age. She lived in a room besides the landing in Relax Inn managed by the three brothers. Mukul observed: "Their mother was the oldest woman I had seen for a very long time. She had dull silver hair and a pale, freckled skin. She was dressed in a cream cotton sari and a woollen shawl, and lay on a low bed, her mottled hands extruding from the bleached mull coverlet on the quilt. Faded colourless eyes peered inquisitively from behind black-framed spectacles." (80-81)

During her stay at the foot of the mountains, Gokhale came in contact with many old and wrinkled faces. In *The Book of Shadows*, she has described the hill people. First of all she describes the caretaker of the house where Rachita Tiwari comes to stay. Lohaniju had unnaturally large ears which made him look like an elf or a character from Star Trek. Lohaniju was fond of telling stories particularly about the old house. When he told the stories his voice became deeper and more dramatic than his everyday voice. Rachita gives us the full details about Lohaniju: "Lohaniju's stories have beguiled me as long as I can remember. His quicksilver tongue maintains many rhythms and momentums. He is a virtuoso storyteller, and his technique has perfected itself over the years. His enormous jug ears protrude at alarming angles from behind his long mutton-chop side whiskers. Whenever he is about to embark upon one of his stories his left ear begins to twitch, and he tugs at the small gold hoops which glisten on his ear lobes. 'That's my twin—my shadow double telling me not to stray from the truth !' he explains and for the duration of the story his left index finger remains ringed through the gold hoop to stop his jug ear from twitching." (12)

Namita Gokhale, in the author's note, has written that she lived in the house she has written about. Hence she has closely observed the hill people, their physical features as well as their natures, clothes and occupations. In the novel she wrote that the hill folk are hard working and enthusiastic when they are working but when they divert their attentions, it was very difficult to make them work. They are not dependable but on the other hand the women folk are more dependable, sturdy and cheerful. William James Cockerell describes the sister of the Bhotiya coolie: "Unlike her brother, who was dark-coloured and rather hideous in appearance, the sister was fair, with red cheeks and a sun-tanned complexion. She had, moreover, the most piercing eyes, with finely arched eyebrows. One eyelid drooped shut a little more than the other, giving a comical roguish expression to her countenance. She had, as did others of her race, a frame capable of endurance and agility, and she could lift the most awesome loads upon her strong back with a lithe and easy grace." (50-51)

The novelist has used the method of comparison between Bhotiya coolie and his sister to highlight her features. Her brother was dark-coloured with ugly features and on the other hand, she was fair with red cheeks. She was enduring and possessed agility. Further we are informed that the Bhotiya girl had "childish enthusiasm" and "carried in her every movement an unhampered, unquestioning freedom; she was a pagan to the core." (51)

Then we have the mystical description of the Mai, one of the 'power' women wandering in the hills dressed in black rags, usually seen in the hill region. Holy madness dripped from their eyes. They are also addicted to bhanj. Rachita saw the Mai wander into the garden. Rachita was curious to know about her and watched her movements carefully. She found her to be mysterious. She observed: "I saw her from the upstairs window as she wandered into the garden, a tall gaunt figure, a skeleton almost, her dirty dishevelled hair covering her drooping breasts. There was something compelling and powerful about her, a dignity in her nakedness and vulnerability. She had a vacant smile and very strong white teeth. She was smiling to herself, at the mountains, at the sky above." (194)

Namita Gokhale meticulously describes the characters in her next novel *Shakuntala: The Play of Memory*. She takes help of animal imagery to describe Kamalini, the handmaiden. Srijan, Shakuntala's husband had brought back Kamalini after one of his travels. Shakuntala felt insecure in her presence. She closely observed her not, missing minute details: "She was standing by the doorway as I entered. Something about her, her clothes perhaps, reminded me of the peacock-feather fan I had received as a gift. With her elongated neck and tall, arching figure she looked like a crane in flight. Her eyes, when they met mine, were like a serpents." (57) Further she observed: "Her eyebrows were curved like a strung bow. Her large, cold eyes, framed by thick upturned lashes, could be described as almond shaped or like the fish that lurked in the waters of the Ganga, depending on which poetic style one preferred. Her nose was long but slim, and two glittering nose rings adored the perfectly shaped curve of her nostrils. Her lips were large and sensuous, her neck a proud column. She was like a high spirited stallion or an unfolding lotus bud." (65)

Shakuntala then describes her brother Guresvara, a scholar and mendicant. He was dressed in holy clothes and followed the rules of monastic discipline strictly. Looking at him, Shakuntala felt cleansed of her doubts and fear. According to her: "My brother's robes were dyed the deep ochre of a mendicant's clothes. His feet were callused from years of consistent walking. His head was shaven except for the tuft of his bundled up topknot. The afternoon sun streamed in from the west, and cast an effulgence around him, a halo of saffron and gold." (SH, 71)

Guresvara had a soothing effect on Shakuntala but she was enchanted by Nearchus with whom she later runs away. She met him by the river, when she had gone to worship the sacred stone blessed by gods in the river Ganga. Having lived at the foot of the Himalayas, Gokhale could never forget the sacred river. She was shocked to find him there as she was all alone. She looked at him and found that he was not dressed like the men she knew. Looking at him she knew instinctively that he had reached there after travelling far and wide. She gets attracted towards him: "He is short, with muscular thighs and stocky calves and the curliest hair I have ever seen, and he is dressed differently from all the men I know: sandals with upturned toes are strapped to his ankles, and a short tunic is tied at his waist with an elaborate leather belt. He looks utterly carefree, reckless and happy; his square, firm face holds a baffling merriment, and I know instinctively, that he has travelled for long and through many worlds to be here. He smiles at me. I am enchanted by his smile." (109)

Nature plays a significant role in the fiction of Namita Gokhale. The human world always interacts with the world of nature in her novels. Nature acts both as a consoling agent as well as a disturbing presence. It provides solace to the characters by taking them away from the world of pain and suffering and at the same time makes them conscious of the grim existential realities. There is a constant interaction between the inner world of the protagonist and the outer world of nature. Nature acts as a symbol of life, hope and destruction.

Namita Gokhale is herself a Kumaoni by birth. Born in Lucknow in 1956, she spent her early childhood in Nainital. She has closely observed the various aspects of nature and could interpret its impact on human mind and life effectively.

In her novels we find nature in its myriad forms performing different roles. In her first novel *Paro: Dreams of Passion* nature plays a very small role. Priya was in love with B.R., her boss. She recollects her first kiss at Marine Drive, which was vast, ugly and compulsive like the vast sea. She yielded immediately to his advances but a part of her held back, observant and clinically detached. Her condition can be compared to the moon hiding behind the clouds and observing the restless sea: "I stared instead at the coy moon hiding behind the white clouds, and watched the restless ocean regurgitate its teeming refuse back onto the black sullen rocks." (3)

Later, when she tried to commit suicide by walking into the sea, she found that the water was friendly and welcomed her in its lap: "For a long time I stood looking at the bay; then, putting my purse down carefully by the shore, I waded in. The water was neither warm nor cold, it was viscous and friendly and it embraced me with a loving sensuality." (141)

For Gudiya in *Gods, Graves and Grandmother*, nature was a living presence and she could communicate with it. As she was feeling alone, nature acted as her companion and guide, at times scolding her when she went wrong. The peepal tree leaves talked to her in sibilant murmur. And when after the summer, before the monsoon, the thunderstorm arrived, the peepal tree flapped its arms and enacted a storm dance: "It was that strange season, that hiatus between summer and the monsoon, when not a leaf stirs and the nights are heavy with stillness and expectation. Then suddenly the air trembles and the thunderstorm awakens like a hundred maddened furies and beats the leaves out of the trees and the crows out of their nests and the dust rises in spirals like spirits from their graves. When the storm broke, my ever-talkative peepal tree grew almost demented with excitement. It flapped its arms and writhed in a sinuous storm dance." (21)

The peepal tree rebuked her by 'shrieking' (22), when she stole a gold coin from grandmother's trunk. And every night as Gudiya fell asleep the peepal tree would begin its seductive song. After Ammi's death, Gudiya was left alone and then the peepal tree took the role of Ammi, soothing and comforting Gudiya in its lap. Gudiya explains her experience: "That afternoon I sat down beneath my peepal tree. It had been raining recently, and the beautifully shaped leaves were replete with sap and spirit. Fanned by the breeze, they waved around sinuously, as though pleased with themselves. A deep, long sigh escaped from within the dense boughs. I felt languorous and relaxed and strangely contented, as though my brow was being soothed by some unseen hand. I felt I was a little girl again, nestling in my Ammi's lap, sheltered by the pallav of her sari. I fell into deep sleep, and when I awoke I was startled to find myself there, alone, in the dusk, as the shadows lengthened." (169)

Then we have the description of the eclipse which is suggestive. The tiny black spot which appeared on the moon grew bigger and bigger, so also the suspicion in the mind of Gudiya, about the renewed intimacy between herself and Ammi: "I looked up at the Moon. The faintest suspicion of a shadow was beginning to crawl about its surface—a tiny black spot that grew bigger and bigger. The birds were getting more excited every second, and their shrill ear-splitting cacophony made it impossible to even hear what Ammi was saying." (51-52)

In *A Himalayan Love Story*, Namita Gokhale has described what was familiar to her—the varied shades of nature during different seasons. She co-relates different activities of nature with changes taking place in the life of her characters. First of all we are told by Parvati that towards the end of bitter winter, she noticed certain changes in her mother's face. She regained the earlier skin colour and the fine nest of wrinkles around her eyes also disappeared. The change of season also has an impact on Parvati. The anxiety and dread which she felt during the cold winter disappeared with the onset of spring. Nature has a soothing effect on her: "The plum and apricot trees were in blossom, and the sky was a clear, triumphant blue. The days were getting warmer, there was something gentle and invigorating about the fragrant March breeze, and a part of the anxiety and dread that I carried like a secret burden seemed to be gradually disappearing with the spring." (13)

As the onset of spring induced the flowering on plum and apricot trees so also the monsoon induced flowering on hydrangeas and tiger lilies. During that season after Lalit's death, she was taken to Ramsay Hospital as she was carrying a child.

The monsoon season was followed by autumn, when all the troubles for Parvati began. The description of the season is vivid and suggestive. It is nothing but a remembrance of the past: "It was when I returned to Wee Nooke that the troubles began. Although it was now autumn, the monsoon clouds had receded and the warm sun shone in a blue cloudless sky, the fog refused to go away. It crept about my forehead, black, smoky, acrid, creating a terrible weather and climate quite its own." (49)

The weather was the premonition of the changes which took place in Parvati's life, as she became a lunatic and was sent to an asylum. But for Mukul, who returns to Nainital for a brief spell, the nature symbolizes the warmth and coziness of homeland. As he was heading towards Nainital, he experienced complete familiarity with the landscape. He could even predict what was going to be the next scene: "There was a complete familiarity in the landscape, each scene reminding me of what was coming next. The sky was like a smudged grey watercolour. My eyes followed the inky cumulonimbus cloud formations towards the most unimaginable shades of green: the young green of the paddy shoots, the deeper colours of the mango trees, the tall lush grass. There was a fulfilment in the earth, in the flooded fields and cavorting parrots, that communicated itself to me even though my tiredness of the day before. I put the window down and smelled the damp earth." (61)

The fulfilment of the earth corresponds to the fulfilment experienced by Mukul on his return to the hills. With the help of colours, Gokhale has presented a perfect picture of nature. Further description also presents Mukul being nostalgic on seeing the myriad forms of nature. When the driver halted at Jeolikote to fill the radiator of the car, Mukul found the fresh spring water gurgling from a lion-headed spout. He sniffed the cool aroma of rain soaked mud. Then he stopped at the toll station outside Nainital. The entire passage describing the nature states the happy state of nature as well as of Mukul. The gentle breeze makes the dahlias swing along with other flowers growing on that part of land. The Monsoon streams were also happily gurgling down the hill and the butterflies were wandering in the sky: "We stopped next at the toll station outside Nainital. Huge heads of dahlias nodded in the breeze. There were marigolds and cosmos and tiger lilies and other sorts of hill flowers the names of which I did not know. Monsoon streams gurgled down the hillside. Butterflies speckled the air." (72)

The Book of Shadows abounds in nature description. The changes in the landscape brought about by the changed season as well as the day which progresses from morning till sunset in the hills is described with telling brevity. Rachita has come to Ranikhet, a town located at the lap of the Himalayas, after an acid attack. She derives the strength to survive from nature. In the beginning of the novel we find her not enjoying the beauty of nature as she was in a disturbed state of mind. But towards the end of the novel we find that, it is the nature which supports her, teaches her the lessons of life, sustains her and induces in her the urge for living. In the beginning of the novel we find her describing the early morning with the sun creeping through the window and birds chirping, thus heralding the arrival of the morning. But she was not in the right frame of mind to enjoy the morning glory: "I awake again as the first light of the morning creeps into the room. The dawn chorus heralds the arrival of day. First a single tinny-voiced bird twitters a brave but not entirely musical welcome to the Sun God. Gradually more voices enter the fray. It could sound lovely if one was in the right frame of mind, but my head is hurting." (32)

But after deriving strength from nature and self-realization, she finds joy in the beauties of nature. The manifestation of nature's beauty is perfectly described: "This is the most beautiful time of the year in our hills. The leaves begin to change colour, and a shadow of red sits upon the hillside. The marigolds are out in full bloom, their rich smells satiate the senses. The tribulations of winter are just around the corner, yet the last snatches of sun-drenched joy still saturate the earth. Marrows sit plumply upon the sloping roofs of village houses, sunning themselves, and tomatoes are dried and preserved for the sunless winter. Corn hangs by the eaves of Lohaniju's cottage, as do garlands of bright red chillies. The Himalayas gleam brightly in the warm clear sunlight, and when the first snows fall in the high reaches of the mountains, powdering the peaks with an added glow, there is something breathtaking and stupendous in their beauty. It is a time to harvest, to conserve, to await a trial of strength with the elements. It is a time of joy and resolution." (BS, 218-219)

William Cockerell, the missionary who built the house in which Rachita lives was of the opinion that the extreme climatic conditions of the Indian subcontinent were hostile for stable growth of civilization. The summers discourage growth but with the first shower of rains the vegetation gets encouragement for thriving: "In the searing summer months not a blade of green grass is to be seen, and the ground is scorched, scarred, and baked. When the first rains arrive, all nature is transformed. The parched earth gives way to the richest green. After the downpour the sun comes out in all its strength under the combined action of heat and moisture, every conceivable form of vegetation thrives vigorously, as, alas, does an infinite variety of pestilential insect life." (41)

Further William Cockerell compares the England autumn with Indian autumn and feels that God pervades all nature. He writes: "It was now the fair month of October, which in those hills is different from an English autumn. The copious monsoon rains had enriched and rejuvenated the soil, and a verdant green blanketed the hills. The heavens were deep and startlingly blue, a sort of rich cobalt colour unknown in England. Against this backdrop rose the noble snow-mountains of the Himalayan range, brilliant in the mellow sunshine; reminders to the human soul of the pervading presence of God." (48)

In *Shakuntala: The Play of Memory* the writer has given vivid description of the months. All the changes taking place due to changed season are presented with minutest details. The writer has successfully painted the word picture with the blooming flowers, the vegetation, the birds and the sky because she had herself seen it many times in the past. Shakuntala was married in the month of Magh. She describes the activities undertaken by the people keeping in tune with the weather: "In the month of Magh the skies are clear, although the days are windy. The people in the hills fly parchment kites adorned with tails of straw and thin strips of cloth. The breeze holds them, lifts them up until they soar high with the hawks and kestrels." (38)

Later, when Shakuntala was on death bed, looking at the kites flying in the sky, she guessed that it was again the month of Magh. The nature reminded her that she was married to Srijan in this month but that was the thing of past. She had broken the marriage vows by running away with Nearchus. And now she was left to die. The fluttering kite brought back the memories of her marriage: "The sky was sometimes grey, sometimes blue, like the colour of Nearchus's eyes. A black kite fluttered far among the clouds. Perhaps it was once again the month of Magh, the month in which I had been married. A striped squirrel came up and examined me with cautious eyes. A mina burrowed in the mud for grains. A large lustrous crow hopped over and perched itself by my head. It was time for me to die." (193)

Shakuntala also describes the month of Chaitra, when forest trees burst with blossoms and the grass glowed with verdant green. The Ganga flowed far below like a silver coloured rope. It was during this month that Shakuntala probably conceived their child. She describes the beauty of Chaitra: "It was late in the month of Chaitra. The forest trees were bursting with blossom. Laburnums blazed against a sharp blue sky. Sheets of bakul flowers lay scattered at my feet. The summer would be upon us soon, but at the moment the grass glowed with the peculiar verdant green of late spring. The smell of earth reminded me of Srijan's skin, so I lay down and breathed deeply of the fragrance of the soil. An eagle was circling above. A Mountain bird broke the air in gentle swoops and dives. I had climbed high up the hill. The almost vertical slope was covered with trees and vines and creepers. The Ganga, far below me, was a shining rope of silver." (91-92)

Thus, it is observed that Namita Gokhale has nostalgic recollections from the past. She displays a fine penchant for creating beautiful word pictures through memory. The descriptions of places, persons and nature are replete with minute details. It displays her fine sense of observation, retention and recollections. Namita Gokhale becomes what Raja Rao calls a true 'Upasaka' in having a strong desire to communicate and in achieving mastery over the language to communicate effectively and forcefully: "Unless the author becomes an 'Upasaka' and enjoys himself in himself (which is 'Rasa') the eternality of the sound (Sabda) will not manifest itself and so you cannot communicate either and the word is nothing but a cacophony."[8]

In her works she has dealt with the cities like Delhi and Mumbai on one hand and the picturesque beauty of the Himalayas on the other hand. She lives in Delhi and visits Mumbai quite often and has spent her early childhood in Nainital. These are the places that she minutely observed all around her from her childhood to her womanhood. She has imparted universal appeal to the scene, landscapes, men and women, customs and traditions of these places.

Namita Gokhale displays extraordinary sensibility which is like as Henry James points out while discussing artist and the artistic process, "a kind of huge spider-web of the finest silken threads suspended in the chamber of consciousness, and catching every air-borne particle in its tissue."[9] She gives vivid details of men, women, places and nature, and in the process she subtly suggests the peculiarities involved.

In her first two novels she has depicted the urban setting with descriptions of offices, houses, streets, cremation ground etc. While in her remaining novels, the hills are depicted with their houses, streets, temples, mysterious places etc. She has also given us the details of the people belonging to these places. She gives the details about their physical features, clothes, jewellery and even their habits. Then we have picturesque word painting of nature, the hills, sea, flowers, trees, seasons, sunrise, eclipse etc. Nature is not just the background of her novels, but a leading character. Sometimes it exercises an influence on the course of events colouring the mood and shaping the disposition of human beings.

NOTES

1. Namita Gokhale, "Nainital," *The Penguin Book of Indian Journeys*. New Delhi: Penguin India, 2001, p. 226.
2. *Ibid.*
3. Qaiser Zoha Alam, "Namita Gokhale's *Gods, Graves and Grandmother*," *Indian Writing in English*, ed. Manmohan K. Bhatnagar, New Delhi: Atlantic, 1998. p. 193.
4. Namita Gokhale, p. 229
5. Namita Gokhale, at http: //www.lifepositive.com
6. E.M. Forster, *Aspects of the Novel*. London: Edward Arnold, 1945. p. 64.
7. M.E. Derret, *The Modern Indian Novel in English*. Brussels: University Library, 1996. p. 91.
8. Raja Rao, "The Writer and the World," *The Literary Criticism*, Vol. VIII, No. I, Winter, 1965.
9. James, Henry. *The House of Fiction*, ed. Leon Edel, London: Rupert Hart Davis, 1957. p. 31.

Narrative Technique

Novel is undoubtedly one of the most powerful and characteristic expressions. As R.K. Dhawan asserts: "The novel is the readiest and most acceptable way of embodying experiences and ideas in the context of our time."[1]

The manner in which to write a good novel, however, remains highly debatable. Many modern critics believe that in the past too much attention was paid to the story or plot overlooking psychological aspects. Some modern novelists have written novels that are experimental and far removed from the traditional story—telling methods. According to Somerset Maugham, these writers who are dubbed anti-novelists, "consider the telling of a story for its own sake as a debased form of fiction."[2] The principal features of the anti-novelists, according to Paul Varghese, are "lack of an obvious plot, diffused episode, minimal development of character; detailed surface analysis of objects, repetitions; experiments with vocabulary, punctuation and syntax, variations of time sequence, alternative endings and beginnings."[3]

The novelists view life with a keen perception, sharp sensibility, an acute sense of observation and a fine sensitivity. They show a deep insight into human nature and at the same time they catch the epiphanies of life in their work. Hence, the narrative technique employed by the novelists is also gaining importance. There is gradual increase in the different methods of story telling but plain narrative is still the most common method employed by the novelist who is omnipresent and omniscient in this type of writing. There are several major techniques that novelists employ to make their novels rich in meaning and rewarding to the reader, including point of view, style, and symbolism. Novelists also use a number of minor devices such as figurative language, humour, imagery and irony.

The point of view determines the limitations and freedoms that the author has in presenting the plot and theme to the readers. Readers will experience a book differently depending on whether they know everything that is occurring in the story and all the characters' thought or they have a more limited perspective, such as knowing only what one particular character knows. Hence, selection of point of view is the most important decision the author must make.

A novelist's style is the approach the writer takes in putting together words, phrases, sentences, and paragraphs. Style can determine the pace at which the story is told and how directly the author relates the story to the reader. Many novelists deepen the meaning of their stories by employing symbolism, the use of objects or ideas as symbols that represent abstract concepts. With symbols authors can write scenes that deepen the reader's understanding of the theme of novel. This occurs because the symbols have an unspoken meaning beyond their immediate presence in the story. Symbolism thus allows the author to address controversial matters, such as political or religious issues, without openly discussing these subjects.

Novelists also use many other literary devices including imagery, irony and humour. By using these devices, writers avoid the need to state every piece of information they wish to convey. Instead, the literary devices give readers the opportunity to discover by themselves the layers of meaning in a novel.

Namita Gokhale has considered for her characters people among whom she lived and moved. She has used various techniques to make her novels appealing to the readers. She has experimented with bringing together words, phrases, sentences, and paragraphs while describing the feelings and experiences of her characters.

Namita Gokhale has used various modes of expression in her novels. She has used first-person narrative and flash-back technique so as to serve her specific purpose effectively. First-person narrative is a narrative mode in which a story is narrated by one character who, explicitly refers to himself or herself in the first-person who is using words and phrases involving "I" (referred to as the first-person singular) and / or "we" (the first-person plural). This allows the reader or audience to see the point of view including opinions, thoughts, and feelings only of the narrator, and of no other characters. In some stories, first-person narrators may refer to information they have heard from the other characters, in order to try to deliver a larger point of view.

The first-person narrative enables the writer to impart a disinterested and objective view of the character: "Who can have his own identity so much separately as from other men and women in the book as from the author himself and reader only what he can hear, think or feel."[4]

Many Indian writers like Mulk Raj Anand, Arun Joshi, Shashi Deshpande have adopted this mode of narration. Namita Gokhale has also used the technique of first-person narrative in all her novels. The novel *Paro: Dreams of Passion* is the succulent tale of a tall, sexy, green-eyed, gin-drinking temptress named Paro and is narrated by the observant Priya, who records not only the commissions and omissions of her friend but also her own. The novel is presented as a confessional account of the narrator's own experiences and those of her friend Paro. It is a kind of "vindication" (3) of what she had seen, heard and felt. It started, we are told, as "a sort of confessional, a diary, which eventually became this thing, this novel." (120)

The narrator claims to have had an instinct for truth and made it a point to see things as they were and not as they should have been or one would pretend they were. The book is the outcome of a sincere effort on her part to sort out past experiences and to find a cathartic relief: "So it is that I am sitting here, many years later, still trying to lay their ghosts, banish their tyrannical mythologies, it is to be a therapeutic experience, an old fashioned catharsis, an enema. I shall vomit out my malice and envy and adoration." (25)

Gokhale's next novel *Gods, Graves and Grandmother* deals with the story of "a courtesan" Ammi, who was a Muslim by religion. She is thrown out of her 'Kotha' and finds herself without any money in a Delhi slum. Gudiya, the granddaughter of Ammi is the narrator of the novel and tells the story in the first-person with frankness and candour and often in a brutally straight- forward manner. To quote a few examples:

> "After mother left, after she ran away with Riyasuddin Rizvi." (11)
>
> "Ever since Riyasuddin Rizvi had decamped with my mother" (38)
>
> "my skin, the pale-gold skin some Afghan forebear or firangi customer had endowed me with." (14)
>
> She thinks of "the Englishman who might have been my father." (59)
>
> "I did not even know who my father was, and neither, for a fact, did my mother or grandmother." (104)

Gudiya refers to her mother as her "wicked waylaid mother." (28) While telling about the harsh realities faced by her grandmother and her struggle for existence, she also tells us about the people who came in contact with the temple established by Ammi.

A Himalayan Love Story is divided into two parts. The narrator of the first part is Parvati, daughter of a poor neglected widow, growing up in Jeolikote, a popular tourist halt in U.P. The second part of the novel is narrated by Mukul, the student of Parvati's uncle, her mother's step-brother, Hiranand Joshi. Mukul is the favourite student of Hiranand Headmaster and the only beneficiary of the old man's last will.

Set in the backdrop of the Nandadevi and its contiguous hill ranges, not far from the Himalayan retreat of Ranikhet, *The Book of Shadows* consists of two parallel narratives. One is by Rachita

Tiwari, who is teacher of English literature. She is trying to re-invent her zest for life in a lonely hilltop bungalow after recovering from an acid attack by the enraged sister of her fiancé, who had committed suicide. The other narrator is a ghost which had haunted the house for over a hundred years, watching and chronicling its bloody history. A portion of the novel also deals with Rachita having a chance insight into the history of the house, when she goes through the journal of an English missionary who had occupied it over century ago. This history is narrated by the missionary, William James Cockerell.

In *Shakuntala: The Play of Memory*, the protagonist Shakuntala is the narrator telling the story in first-person. The novel is a tale of Shakuntala of the northern mountains—spirited, imaginative, but destined like her legendary namesake to suffer "the samskaras of abandonment."

Flashback is a scene in the novel which is set at the time earlier than narrative. It is the retrospective method of narration where the characters muse and recollect the events of the past. This technique of narration is adopted by novelists like Anita Desai, Arun Joshi, Bhabani Bhattacharya, Nayantara Sahgal etc

Namita Gokhale also uses this mode of telling the story partly, through flash-backs. She uses this technique in all her novels. She describes the situations or the turning point in her character's life long after they actually took place.

Paro: Dreams of Passion begins with the information about Priya writing a novel. Then she goes into past to narrate the circumstances which led her to write about Paro, B.R. and herself. Priya, coming from a typical middle-class background, idolizes Paro and B.R. and imitates Paro whom B.R. marries. Hence, she writes about them. The novelist again comes in the present on page 121 but again moves into past when Priya narrates how her diary writing was discovered by Paro and Suresh, her husband. We are brought back into the present from page 126 till the end of novel which is also the end of Priya's novel.

Gods, Graves and Grandmother opens up with Gudiya telling us that her mother had left her and her grandmother, to fend for themselves. But her resourceful grandmother with the help of a marble slab and five rounded river stones, all these stolen from nearby area, builds up a shrine. Instead of narrating the story further she takes a retrospective step to describe the circumstances in which they reached the Delhi slum. From chapter three onwards the narrative moves into present.

The second part of the novel *A Himalayan Love Story* begins with Mukul, the narrator of this part receiving the letter from Hiranand Headmaster bequeathing everything he had to Mukul. He sets out for Nainital. In chapter titled 'Pitaji Masterji,' the reader is told by Mukul about his family background and how he came in contact with Parvati in Wee Nooke.

The novel *The Book of Shadows* begins with Rachita sitting by the window of the house in the Himalayan retreat of Ranikhet. She is all alone in the house. She describes the circumstances which brought her to this house. The novelist uses flash- back to tell about Rachita's past, her days in college as an English literature teacher, Anand's suicide and the acid thrown by his sister on her face damaging it. Then we have Rachita reading the journal of William James Cockerell and the story told by the ghost about the house in flash-back.

In *Shakuntala: The Play of Memory*, on the ghats of Kashi the most ancient of cities, a woman confronts memories that have pursued her through birth and rebirth. In this life she recalls, she was Shakuntala of the northern mountains. Shakuntala's life and her journey culminating into reaching her destination Kashi is narrated by the novelist using the flash-back technique. Namita Gokhale adopts the retrospective narration to recollect the events of the past life of her characters.

Namita Gokhale has used a large number of Indian words in her novels like other Indian writers. This is to impart the Indian touch. A translation of these words in English would not have brought the rich connotation attached to these words. We have in her novels Indian names for flowers, animals, trees, food items, addresses, clothes, things, names of the days, religious rituals etc.

In *Paro: Dreams of Passion* we have the following Indian names: Chameli, raat-ki-rani, kamardhani, agarbatti, jhaadoo, rakhi, aayah, sahib, memsahib, bahu, bhaiyya, barsati, jhola, aandhi, Lakshmi, pan, papad, pakoda, moongphali, laddoos, mujra, tankha, lafda, yaar etc.

In *Gods, Graves and Grandmother* we have: Mogra, chameli, peekdan, hookah, paan-daan, saropa, lota, dhobi, Allah, Behenji, zamindar, Tabalchi, baisaheb, mamaji, achkan, kurta, chunni, pardah, shastras, Poornamashi, Amavasya, nankhatai, mithai, laddoos, halva-puri, Rahu, gaja-kesari-yoga, muhurtam, kanyadan, mangalashtaka etc.

In *A Himalayan Love Story* there are numerous Indian words: Chameli, choolah, pateela, surahi, beedi, chimta, lota, janeyu, daayans, chaprasi, goonda, makdi, kurta, khadi, Gandhi topi, pyjamas, aloo ki guthe, aloo ka pani, aloo tomato, aloo matar, dal, roti, khichdi, jawla, khus-khus, samosas, jalebis, potato tikkis, kachauris, dal-bhat, dalmoth etc.

We also find use of Indian words by Namita Gokhale in *The Book of Shadows*. They are: chil, chir, sagad, choti, janeu, chunni, damru, hurka, dandi, thali, agnikund, hurkiyas, ghagra, memsahib, ghasyarans, bitiya, dayans, mukhiya, Vanbhanjika, Kagbhushandi, Shaktins, Mais, sanyasins, jagar, prasad, pithya etc.

In *Shakuntala: The Play of Memory* we find the following Indian words: Indragopa, amalaka, ashwagandha, tulsi, kantakari, bakul, harsingar, pathya, madhumalti, mogra, chameli, anjana, alta, harial, kokila, dhoomketu, Shalabhanjika, Saptarishis, Dhruva-tara, Rishi, Mahasamant, mahout, sartha, modaka, ladduka, amavasya, ravivara, purabias, mriga, karma, aarti, karmapatha, jnana-patha, Brahma-sutras, Ritusamhara, agnicayana, sutras, godhuli, mrighastin etc.

Namita Gokhale has also used Indian expressions. In fact, she exploits the two codes, Hindi-English to create the necessary impact. According to Meenakshi Mukherjee: "Earlier English was the language of public discourse, of higher education. It is only for a section of those born in the 1950, and after that, English is a first language, sometimes their only language. They display a careless intimacy with English, which enables them to play with it."[5]

A few examples of Indian expressions used by her in her novels are cited below. In *Paro: Dreams of Passion* we have Paro saying "Ab tamasha khatam" (28) when crowd gathers on Bucky's car hitting a family of three. "Asli memsahib hai," they would say fervently. (34) In *Gods, Graves and Grandmother* we have: "Allah gives and allah takes away" (10) uttered by Riyasuddin Rizvi when he gives a maroon leather pouch to Ammi. "Arre Rama Rama Rama" (12) In *A Himalayan Love Story* the following expressions are used: "Koi baat nahi" (40) said Lalit's brother Raju on seeing Parvati sleeping alone in the kitchen instead of her and Lalit's bedroom. Again, we have "choti-choti baaten" (40) In *The Book of Shadows* she uses: "Maunam sarvam sadhanam" (13) Lohaniju said to Rachita when he was referring to the information about the work:

Para gharua bhoot roon
Je chan cha saboot duen (28)

In *Shakuntala: The Play of Memory* there are expressions like: "Like a dhoomaketu" said Shakuntala about the past life memory which still persists like the tail of dhoomketu. Again, "A profusion of amalaka, tulsi, Kantahari" (7) Namita Gokhale has also used in her novels some hybrid words. To cite a few:

In *Paro: Dreams of Passion*, there are expressions like "Delhi-wallahs" (104) and "Thelawala" (13) In *Gods, Graves and Grandmother*, we have: "tea-shopwallah" (4) and "Chaiwallah" (60) In *A Himalayan Love Story*, we have: "Khaditopi Independence-walas" (118) and "Club walas" (123)

Namita Gokhale has used collective nouns abundantly to give us an idea of quantity. In *Paro: Dreams of Passion* we have an incident when on one night, Paro and Lenin had a massive fight. They went to Priya's house and Paro bolted herself in the room. Suresh asked Priya to make coffee till Paro calmed down. When Priya entered the kitchen, she found many cockroaches, whom she refers to as "a sea of cockroaches." (55) The cockroaches had come out of their hiding places as it was dark in the kitchen. Other examples are "convulsion of tears" (54), "circlet of night flowers" (81), "garbage heaps" (81), "A fretwork of fine lines" (106) etc.

In *Gods, Graves and Grandmother*, we are told by Gudiya that one fine morning clusters of bananas had miraculously materialized on banana trees planted by Phoolwati. Suddenly monkeys appeared there. She calls them "an army of chattering monkeys" (36). The expression gives an idea of the number of monkeys. Few more examples are "handfuls of uncooked rice" (37), "pile of rubble" (57), "a basketful of coconut shells" (79), "packets of coconut" (83) etc.

In *A Himalayan Love Story*, Parvati's house in Jeolikote did not have electricity so they had "a couple of bottle lamps" (7) to light the house. Then we also have examples of collective nouns as "heaps and mounds of rice" (11), "heap of pine cones" (14), "crores and crores of rupees" (205).

Collective nouns are abundantly used in *The Book of Shadows*, Rachita found in the old house "heap of old comics" (17) to read during night as she could not sleep. Further we have bag full of cassettes and discs" (27), "a can of baked beans" (29), "parade of butterflies" (42), "clusters and clouds of flies" (136), "bunch of sweat-peas" (163), "crowd of people" (199), "a sea of yellow butterflies" (227).

In *Shakuntala: The Play of Memory*, Kamalini, the handmaiden was asked by Shakuntala to braid her hair. Kamalini brings "a handful of dhatri flowers" (66) to decorate the braid. Few more examples are, "army of marching blue insects" (6), "a handful of disciples" (12), "a handful of fragrant white jasmine" (171) etc.

Namita Gokhale has powerful command over language. With the help of appropriate words she is able to revive or re-create a situation. She is a keen observer of men, women and nature around her. She has woven her observations in the form of words and presented live and vivid descriptions of nature, people, natural phenomenon and places. We find various examples of her descriptive power spread across her novels.

In *Paro: Dreams of Passion*, Priya gives a graphic description of B.R.'s hair at the age of forty-six and compares it with his previous condition of hair: "I see him as he is now—and he is very different. His hair, which to my besotted eye had as much vitality in its every black root as in his every magical gesture or action, is now plastered vainly over his balding forehead. He is prematurely grey at forty-six, and the salt-and-pepper hair on his hirsute softly undulating chest is always exposed all the way to the swollen belly-button." (2)

In *Gods, Graves and Grandmother*, Namita Gokhale has vividly described the activities taking place in and around the temple set up by grandmother. Gudiya gives us the description of the aarti performed in the temple in the evening. She also tells us about the impact it had on the passersby: "In the evening we lit an earthen lamp at the shrine and performed aarti. Shambhu of the tea stall produced a large luminous conch shell from which he coaxed an awesome and angry wail. Two strangers stopped by on their way home from office. They clapped and kept time as grandmother clanged the brass bell that had magically materialized and now hung like some mystical fruit from the branches of the peepal tree." (2)

Namita Gokhale gives a perfect picture of the activities of beggars around the temple. This is a typical Indian situation. The description exhibits her keen observation of the people and places around her. The passage also gives us a glimpse into human nature. We are told that beggars around the temple would be busy plucking nits from each other's hair and scratching their bodies but when a rich man came to the temple they immediately assumed the posture of distress: "Encouraged by the crowds, a temporary colony of beggars had mushroomed outside the temple. They seemed scarcely human. They were more like monkeys, plucking nits from each other's hair and scratching themselves indecorously, except when they sighted a prospective donor, in which case they expeditiously assumed a posture of extreme distress and desolation." (84)

A Himalayan Love Story also has lively description of landscape, people, nature, natural phenomenon and typical Indian situations. Mukul was heading towards Nainital. He experienced familiarity with the landscape and could predict the next scene. The earth looked saturated with greenery: "There was complete familiarity in the landscape, each scene reminding me of what was coming next. The sky was like a smudged grey watercolour. My eyes followed the inky cumulonimbus cloud formations towards the most unimaginable shades of green: the young green of the paddy shoots, the deeper colours of the mango trees, the tall lush grass. There was a fulfilment in the earth, in the flooded fields and cavorting parrots, that communicated itself to me even through my tiredness of the day before." (61)

The novelist also describes the typical Indian situation found in the Indian household. One of the corners of the room was devoted to god. It was a worship place where all gods are cramped in the form of coloured pictures and idols. Along with this there was the presence of all paraphernalia necessary for worshipping God. Mukul went to meet Mohan Mischief's mother in her room and minutely observed the surroundings: "All around her, brilliantly coloured pictures of gods and goddesses emblazoned the walls. Rama and Sita jostled with Krishna. There was a calendar of Lord Shiva at his meditations, entwined with serpents, and the Ganga spouting fitfully from his locks. An outdated calendar had Parvati, or at least I assumed it was her, plucking flowers from a celestial garden, surrounded by handmaidens." (81)

It is a humorous portrayal where we find that gods jostle with each other for supremacy. All the calendars having pictures of gods and goddesses are meticulously preserved although they have become old and one has to keep guessing about the deities. Further Mukul describes the small wooden mandir which again was crowded with deities: "On the floor near Ija's bed was a small wooden mandir, like a doll's house. It sheltered a Shiva linga, a Ganesh and several other deities. Before it rested a brown cloth—bound *Ramcharitmanas*, a conch shell, a brass prayer bell with a carved Nandi bull upon its handle and an aarti. Fruits and flowers were piled on a plate. A damp, musky smell hung about the room, the smell of incense and shut windows and old age." (81)

Namita Gokhale's *The Book of Shadows* is replete with description of hills, the people and things associated with it. This is because she herself belonged to the Kumaon region and also lived in the house she has written about for few days. Her descriptions give us information about hills, hill people, animals, plants and the prevalent customs there: "The exhausted taxi wheezed and coughed towards the hilltop, through the winding kuccha road with its stones and boulders and exposed tree-roots. The splats of cow dung that marked our path seemed almost reassuring, indicating the presence of domestic animals. Two giggling *ghasyarans* in bright blue petticoats, with sickles in their hands and bundles of fodder balanced on their pretty heads, met us as we passed. They stared after us curiously. I'm sure they hadn't seen a car in these parts for years." (8-9) The passage describes the typical Indian situation observed in the hilly region. The roads are not tarred, hence stones, boulders and exposed tree roots are visible. Cowdung is splattered on the road and then we have the wonderful description of the ghasyarans who are simple and innocent.

In one of the passages Namita Gokhale gives us the information about the Bhotiya dogs found in the hills. First she has described them as types and later on she moves to the individual characteristics. She tells us that these dogs are brave, fearless and loving, surviving in the mountain habitat. The novelist displays her love for hills when she goes to the extent of saying that the Bhotiyas sanctify the place where they live. Rachita tells us: "Bhotiyas are the most wonderful dogs in the world, they are brave and fearless and loving, but they don't survive in the plains, they belong to these mountains, and in many senses, these mountains belong to them. This is not just a charming inversion, there's more to it than that. This breed shares some symbolic strength with the soil and stones of our mountains. Bhotiyas sanctify the places where they live." (BS, 25)

The novel *Shakuntala: The Play of Memory* has also lively description of the meandering river, the hills and the sky in the month of Ashad: "Meandering, the holy river winds through the month of Ashad. The hills gaze towards the distant plains. Trembling blue-green, the sky turns the colour of a lotus leaf. The still, late-summer haze holds the first premonitions of thunder." (5)

There is a lively picture of the nature during the month of Magh as witnessed by dying Shakuntala. The nature is present with all its hue and colour: "The sky was sometimes grey, sometimes blue, like the colour of Nearchus's eyes. A black kite fluttered far among the clouds. Perhaps it was once again the month of Magh, the month in which I had been married. A striped squirrel came up and examined me with cautious eyes. A mina burrowed in the mud for grains. A large lustrous crow hopped over and perched itself by my head. It was time for me to die." (193)

Namita Gokhale has also depicted the native situations including conditions of the hospitals, the habit of people to interpret things as per their own convenience to give a mystical touch and literal translation of vernacular language into English. To cite a few examples:

In *Paro: The Dreams of Passion* we are told by Priya about her abortion. She refers to the ambulance, nursing home, and the doctor present on duty: "The sheets of our sturdy double bed were stained red with murderous congealed blood; I went in a rickety ambulance, dark as the night, to the noisy nursing home, where the bored doctor on duty aborted me." (70)

In *Gods, Graves and Grandmother* we are told how after Ammi's death people were eager for a miracle which was not taking place. Gudiya drapes the body of Ammi with her old amber chunni sequined with silver, embroidered with gold. Since there were no miracles occurring, Pandit Kailash Shastry invented one. He told the devotees that the chunni had mysteriously draped itself around Ammi and that it was a gift from Goddess Durga: "Meanwhile the crowds surged on, hungry for miracles. As none had occurred, Panditji expeditiously decided to announce one. The chunni, he explained, to a few close devotees, was a funerary gift from the Goddess Durga, Ma Shakti herself. It had mysteriously draped itself around the departed saint even as mourners milled around her mortal remains. The chunni was saffron, the sacred colour—it was a sign, a blessing, a certain case of direct intervention from the cosmic powers." (77)

In *A Himalayan Love Story* Rakesh Kumar, the purveyor of carburettors narrated how the bus he was travelling in carried his bag containing fifteen thousand rupees leaving him behind. Mukul was shocked by his rhetoric when he referred to the bus as 'sea' instead of 'she': "I set off for Nainital this morning," he continued in an adenoidal wheeze. "For pleasure and joy of walking and to pay deposit for a shop. My sister-in-law is wishing to open showroom there, a Vimal textile showroom. At Moradabad, I was under a tree, chewing paan. You understand paan? Yes, betel leaf. As I was thus chewing and discussing with Prithipal Singh, as I was thus engaged in time passing, my bus departed for the hilly place. And, Sir Ji, with her, seated within, my sum total of life savings, fifteen thousand bucks! In a white-and-blue bag of the Pan Am Airlines! Now Sir Ji, sea is in Nainital!" (68)

In the novels of Namita Gokhale we have a realistic reflection of death. She has minutely presented the sufferings of a dying person and a dead body. She also gives her philosophical reflections about death. This is because she has witnessed death from close quarters. She herself had near-fatal encounter with death, when she was suffering from uterus cancer, her mother-in-law died in her arms; her sister-in-law Sunanda Bhandare, Judge of the Delhi High Court succumbed to cancer, and finally her husband Rajiv died in Singapore of cirrhosis of the liver. Her brush with death took deep roots in her psyche.

Gudiya describes the position of dead Ammi. She observes: "I found her lying in bed in an unnatural position. She was curled up in an umbilical pose, one hand a little raised as though warding off attack, an expression of entreaty on her face. A thin stream of dried -up spittle clung by the side of her chin." (73)

Anand's dead body dangling from the ceiling was located by Rachita in *The Book of Shadows*. Namita Gokhale has supplied minute details as to how the body looks when a person commits suicide by hanging himself: "Anand's tongue, the tongue I had known from his kisses, hung lifeless from the corner of his mouth, like in some comic caricature. It leered at me, it jeered my surprise. It was purple and swollen and the spit had not yet dried on it. I could not catch Anand's eye, he was staring with something resembling surprise not at me but the upturned chair beneath him. The curtain stirred and through the still silence of the hot June night I could hear the distant roar of departing traffic echoing like an ocean in my head." (5)

Namita Gokhale has also expressed her view about death through her characters. Parvati in *A Himalayan Love Story* muses on death when she sees the belongings of her dead husband, his shaving cream, shaving brush, nail cutter, his watch, wallet, slippers, and his clothes hanging in the cupboard. She thinks that he is dead but his things remain even after he is gone: "Thinking of this, I can only conclude that death is not final. It is an adversary, an unequal one, and the victors in this battle are rocks and stones. And razors. And wristwatches, even if they have not been wound up, and lie coiled like mortally wounded snakes in steel boxes, next to cheap leather wallets from which the notes have been removed, though not the coins, and squeezed-out tubes of shaving cream. These are my views on mortality." (48)

Another philosophical expression about death is found in her novel *Shakuntala: The Play of Memory*. Shakuntala had been wounded by a charging bull. Her abdomen was injured. She was on the verge of death: "To face death is not as difficult as one might imagine. The main point is that there is very little time. Everything happens in such a rush, so suddenly, that there is no place for terror. Time contracts even as it expands. It becomes irrelevant, as does everything else. There is, at the last frontier, no pain—for the body has its own defence against extreme pain—only a luxurious sense of surrender, of giving up responsibility." (SH, 194)

Gokhale often takes a close look at human eyes before commenting on them. A few instances may be cited as under. In

Paro: Dreams of Passion, Paro remembers her first meeting with B.R. and "her grey-green eyes crinkled in memory." (Paro, 31) Paro, through eyes also expresses her feelings of hatred towards Priya from time to time. When Paro catches Priya and B.R. having dinner together, she would, "Every now and then she would fix a look of contempt and hatred in our direction." (Paro, 43) When Priya goes to Paro's barsati, seeing her, "Her eyes flashed with malice and hatred at the sight of me." (45) Usually, "Paro directed her usual look of pure malice in my direction" (52) or "Paro threw me a look of pure venom." (93)

In *Gods, Graves and Grandmother*, Roxanne Madam's mother, Mrs. Dubash's eyes bored into her as she spoke .Gudiya describes her eyes: "They were old eyes, ringed with wrinkles and glazed over with yellow film, and yet they had a look of humour and cunning and alertness about them." (96)

On Gudiya's third day at Roxanne's house the dogs ran up to her, snarling furiously and she recognized their eyes: "They were canine eyes, brown and excited in pursuit, but they held a blank red glint which stopped me short on my tracks." (98)

Gokhale has presented the details about both human and animal eyes effectively. In *A Himalayan Love Story*, the poet Hasrat Rampuri's eyes become exultant when he would explain Meghdoot. Mukul remembers those eyes: "I remembered Hasrat's pale eyes, grey and exultant, as at a seminar when he would explain the concept of 'Meghdoot' to us." (65-66)

In *The Book of Shadows* we have an exact account of the eyes of Dona Rosa, the inhabitant of the house when the Ghost tells its story. She probably had the intuition of the presence of the ghost or she knew about their world. The ghost saw it in her eyes: "I could see it in her eyes, amber flecked with black, and in that disconcerting look, so direct and yet so deceptively helpless, with which she had turned to the man as he came in. The eyes are important, for the eyes are the highway to the soul. That is where we can be glimpsed, me and my kind, inhabitants of the shadows." (86) Then we are told about the eyes of the pahari escorts and their reactions after receiving money, by the ghost: "The hill men left as phlegmatically as they had come, their shrewd brown eyes lighting up only at the sight of the rupee coins that Captain Wolcott gave them to speed them on their mission." (161-62)

Kamalini, the handmaiden in *Shakuntala: The Play of Memory* was "exotically beautiful woman with cold and mocking eyes." (58) When Shakuntala inquired about the absence of the old cleaning woman, Narangi, the new cleaning woman told her with " eyes dancing with suppressed excitement," (159) that she was dead.

Language is the tool in the hands of the writers to express their feelings, ideas and experiences. As regards the language of her fiction, Namita Gokhale frequently makes experiments. Being an Indian writer, she has to convey through English the vast range of expressions, experiences and observations to the people whose awareness has been conditioned by languages other than English. While doing so, she is confronted, like other Indian English writers, with the problem of handling the English language skillfully. Raja Rao, too, recognized the problem and admitted in his 'Foreword' to *Kanthapura*: "The telling has not been easy. One has to convey in a language that is not one's own the spirit that is one's own. One has to convey the various shades and omissions of a certain thought movement that looks maltreated in an alien language. After language the next problem is that of style. The tempo of Indian life must be infused into our English expression, even as the tempo of American or Irish life has gone into the making of theirs."[6]

In order to overcome this problem, novelists have made different experiments with language. According to Meenakshi Mukherjee, these "experiments can be classified under three heads, experiment in diction (literal translation of idioms), experiments in syntax (changing the structure of sentences) and imagery."[7]

Gokhale has also therefore, taken certain liberties with the normal diction and syntax of English in the process of her creativity. Her novels abound in similes. Some of Gokhale's similes are ordinary and commonplace. In *Paro: Dreams of Passion*, B.R., "allowed himself to be used as a lamp-post or as a letterbox for women to send messages to their husbands through." (40) On being questioned by Suresh regarding the gossip about Priya and B.R., Priya pretended to stammer while telling him that she met B.R. with Paro once and yet, "In my heart, I was as sure and confident as a rock that I could handle Suresh." (44)

In *Gods, Graves and Grandmother* also Namita Gokhale has used number of similes to put forth her point. Gudiya tells us that her grandmother had started believing in God and had started fasting four days a week. She withdrew into some intense and personal confrontation with the idols in the temple. Then "A luminous peace began to float like a cloud over her, distancing her from me." (27) When Gudiya would tread tired legs of Phoolwati with her bare feet, she felt "like a mountaineer, cautiously traversing up her enormous thighs and then back again." (82)

In *A Himalayan Love Story* the similes are apt. After coughing violently Lalit's "face was pale as death." (45) Due to T.B. Lalit had severe bouts of coughing which almost took energy out of his body and his face became pale. The face resembled the dead man's face. About madness, which is quite common in the hills, Mukul observes: "Mental illness runs like a secret rivulet through the genetic pools of Kumaon." (137)

There are number of similes in *The Book of Shadows* to describe various things. Dhayans said to Lohaniju when he went to the forest "in voices as soft as the moonlight." (14) The Dayans wanted Lohaniju to follow them and hence whispered in his ear so that no one could hear them. When Anand pricked his finger, "A tiny droplet of blood, as red as my sari, oozed out of his skin, his living breathing skin." (31)

In *Shakuntala: The Play of Memory* we have numerous similes through which the novelist attempts to convey the intended meaning. Shakuntala tells us, "The Sangha faithful were snoring like ogres." (15) The Buddhist monks were creating noise due to their snoring which was equivalent to the snores of the man-eating giants of fairy tales.

Shakuntala's mother had told her, "never forget, the vessel of your virtue is like the urn of water you balance on your head." (40) Shakuntala had forgiven her mother for being partial towards her brother and she "swallowed those hurts and jealousies like a bitter potion, a medicine which strengthens." (44)

Namita Gokhale has made occasional use of metaphors to put her thoughts before the readers. In *Paro: Dreams of Passion* how the conversation between Priya, Suresh and Lenin was in progress is described. It is said that, "and the conversation too was running on normal rails." (55) Commenting on her mother's behaviour Priya wonders whether her mother was the model for scriptwriter of films or her mother's inflections of love and maternal solicitude had been picked up from "the embryonic dark of the cinema hall." (8) Here the darkness of cinema hall is compared to the darkness in the womb.

In *Gods, Graves and Grandmother* we have Gudiya crying at Roxanne Madam's house remembering her grandmother and the flow of tears is compared to the rapid flow of river. She tells, "A torrent of hot tears was flowing down my cheeks." (87) Phoolwati tells Roxanne angrily "Our Gudiya is not some pet dog or kitten for your Madam to play with and amuse herself." (107) We get a concrete metaphor when the busy Delhi road has been shown as "the river of traffic and diesel fumes." (133)

Describing her problem of numerous pimples, Gudiya says, "My face has sprouted a crop of uncharacteristic pimples." (136)

While on his way to Nainital, in *A Himalayan Love Story* Mukul describes the movement of his car through the waiting traffic, "Our Mercedes effortlessly ploughed through the waiting traffic." (61) Then we have two metaphors to describe Mukul's attraction towards Parvati. He says, "I was an iron filing resisting a magnet, a hurled rock defying gravity." (134)

In *The Book of Shadows*, Rachita compares Mahadevi Verma's poetry with camera obscura, "Mahadevi is a sort of camera obscura, the kind they had in the middle ages, which painters used to reflect the proportions of their subject." (73) Rachita hates flute, she feels, "It's cloying, its creepy, it's crawly, it's crepuscular." (198)

Shakuntala in *Shakuntala: The Play of Memory* tells us that Kamalini's voice was "Melodious, the twanging of a tautly drawn veena string." (58) Shakuntala dreamt, "I was a black buck being chased by a king and his charioteer." (150)

Personification is a device in which animals, plants, elements of nature and abstract ideas are given human attributes. Namita Gokhale in her novels has personified animals, plants and elements of nature by giving them human attributes. Instances of personification abundantly abound in her novels. For the sake of brevity only the following are mentioned.

In *Paro: Dreams of Passion* we have instances of personification. Priya "I walked through the dying lawns and anaesthetized corridors of the hospital," (57) where Paro was admitted after suicide attempt .Here 'dying' and 'anaesthetized' are the words associated with hospitals. The lawns are silent because people are not present on them and the corridors are anaesthetized because the people sitting or standing there are tense and have lifeless, expressionless faces. Paro was sitting on the balcony during mid-afternoon when, "The westerly sun cast a hypnotic reflected glare" (16) and tried to hypnotize her by its rays.

Then we have "silent dining table." (116) Since Suresh was very busy with his advocacy, he had hardly any time to spend with Priya. They met only during weekend parties or across the dinning table for having breakfast or dinner but even during that time they would not talk to each other. Hence the dinning table was silent due to lack of conversation between its occupants.

In *Gods, Graves and Grandmother*, Gudiya tells us, "When the storm broke, my ever-talkative peepal tree grew almost demented with excitement. It flapped its arms and writhed in a sinuous storm dance." (21) The peepal tree is given the attribute of a human as Gudiya many a times felt that it talked to her.

One night Gudiya saw her grandmother leaving the room and Gudiya went behind her. It was a full moon night and the moon "hung suspended complacently over the still slumscape and the tired field." (53) As it was night, the dwellers of the slums were sleeping and those who worked in the fields were also tired and taking rest. Hence, the field is depicted as tired since there was a lot of activity taking place for whole day due to people working there.

In *A Himalayan Love Story* rain has been personified as a human who is angry and furious "An angry drizzle gave way to furious hail storm." (14) Parvati went to the forest to collect firewood. She also collected pine cones. This was opposed by her mother with a resounding slap. She was angry and stubborn. Hence the rain also appeared to be angry and hail storm was furious. After Lalit's death, "His slippers still lie under bed, waiting." (HLS, 47-48) The slippers are personified as a human being waiting for its master.

The house in *The Book of Shadows* is also personified and it was first angry with Rachita for forgetting its love and later tried to soothe her: "It has taken me in, enveloped my hurt. It soothes my hatred, hushes my sorrow. It had been hostile at first, angry that we had forgotten the sanctuary of its love." (7)

The road towards the house was rough. The taxi carrying Rachita is personified. "The exhausted taxi wheezed and coughed towards the hiiltop." (8) Its condition was just like exhausted man who was breathless and coughed due to the dryness of throat after an arduous climb. Rachita was also exhausted.

In *Shakuntala: The Play of Memory*, Shakuntala's mother, by way of personifying the clouds, gives a fine piece of caution to her. When Shakuntala told her mother that she wanted to wander like birds and clouds, her mother said to her that the birds wander for the whole day in search of food but return to their nests and are safe. But the clouds do not return and hence weep in unknown lands in the form of rain: "Remember, Shakuntala," she said, "birds return to their nests at dusk, but clouds must weep their tears unseen in distant lands." (9)

Shakuntala has questions in her mind regarding Kamalini, the handmaiden brought by her husband. She was angry and went to the banks of the river Ganga, where she conferred with the fisherman, Kundan. She looked at the river and felt that the it was a human whose, "anger was gone and she was playful now, a loving, forgiving, easy-going river on a late spring afternoon." (63)

Alliteration is the repetition of a speech sound in sequence of nearby words. Usually the term is applied only to consonants, and only when the recurrent sound begins a word or a stressed syllable within a word. It is a phonological device used to enhance the effect. Namita Gokhale has used alliteration in her novels. A few examples from her novels are cited:

> In *Paro: Dreams of Passion*: "the perfectly tended potted plants, as perfectly tended as the oyster pale nails of his personal secretary." (1) Again, "swallow me up, and swallow my white sandals and my white home-starched Lucknowi sari too." (17)

In *Gods, Graves and Grandmother* there are the following alliterations: "I resolved that someday, somehow, somewhere, I would get even with all of them" (130) and "the hair of an old woman, weaving and wondering through the pall of dust and diesel." (135)

In *A Himalayan Love Story* also Namita Gokhale has made use of alliterations: "The body departs, it is taken away, disposed of, it disintegrates, decomposes, it is gone." (47) Again, "despite the attentions of many diligent dentists," (65)

In *The Book of Shadows* there are following alliterations: "the changed contours of my cheeks," (7) and "their full fragrance flooding the senses" (38)

In *Shakuntala: The Play of Memory* we have a number of alliterations. A few of them are: "the gold and gems and garments" (50); "the sandy soil was stained with blood." (53)

For achieving the rhythmic beauty of a lyric, Namita Gokhale employs the device of repetition which gives incantatory tone to the narrative. Phrases as well as words are repeated. The examples are given below.

In *Paro: Dreams of Passion*: Paro told the crowd "Jao, Jao" (28) to disperse the crowd. Again, Paro told Priya that the crows were going "Caw Caw" (3) in the trees signifying commotion.

In *Gods, Graves and Grandmother* also Namita Gokhale has used this device: Grandmother uttered the words "Chhi chhi chhi!" (16) to show her displeasure when Gudiya insisted on buying a doll for her. When Sundar Pahalwan comes to grandmother's jhuggi to take money, she exclaims "Arre Rama, Rama, Rama," (12) on hearing his words.

In *A Himalayan Love Story* we have: The sound of thunder repeated as 'Da, Da, Da.' (66); The knocking sound on the car window by Rakesh Kumar is repeated to bring out the effect, "rat- a tat-tat, he knocked, rat a tat-tat." (67); Hiranand Headmaster always believed in Mukul and knew that only he would send him letters and then he would say assertingly, "Only

Mukul Nainwal didn't let me down," he would always say, "Only Mukul Nainwal." (98)

In *The Book of Shadows*: Lohaniju ran with full strength and to bring out the gravity of situation, Gokhale has used repetition, "I ran and I ran and I ran." (15). Then Lohaniju described how Airee ate "gobble gobble gobble" (15). In *Shakuntala: The Play of Memory* when Gayatri mantra was being recited by the priest at her brother's Upnayana, her mother closed her ear with her flaxen antariya and said:

> "You can't listen to the mantras," she told me, "or else."
> "Or else what?" I challenged.
> "Or else you'll grow a moustache and no one will marry you." (19)

Then we have the sound of Kokila, the bird, "Kuoo." It would say, "kuoo, kuoo!" (41) to produce a sonorous effect.

One more peculiar feature of Namita Gokhale's language, a characteristic shared by other Indian writers, is that of reduplicating a word with a change of initial sound. Gokhale is not the first to make use of such words. We are reminded of Rushdie's "writing-shaiting," Shobha De's "Independence-shindependence" and Jhabvala's "B.A., P.A." This is a peculiar Indianism and, therefore, according to R.S. Pathak, "adds to the verisimilitude" and "recreates typical Indian ethos."[8]

The novelist may employ this device in various contexts, but the initial purpose is always to infuse colloquialism into the dialogue. For example: In *Paro: Dreams of Passion* we have: "Sinister Minister" (80), "Ha'penny Tu'penny" (91) and "marriage sharriage" (98) In *Gods, Graves and Grandmother* we have: "Madam-Shadam" (90), "philosphy-wilosophy" (120), "palace-walace" (137), "studies-wuddies" (147) and "disco-shisco." (217) In *The Book of Shadows* there are words like: "raggle-taggle" (43), "mumbo-jumbo" (155) and "rag-tag." (159) In *Shakuntala: The Play of Memory* she has used only one such word, "titbit." (152)

Like many other Indian English writers, Gokhale too repeats "and" and the repetition in most cases, heightens the artistic effect. In *Paro: Dreams of Passion* we have: "Then she looked B.R. straight in the eye, her glittering lashes coated with gold and black and venom, and spat, with force and accuracy, into his startled face." (43) Again, "I knitted sweaters and shawls and booties for my unborn child—I embroidered bed sheets and pillowcases and stitched nappies and searched for a suitable ayah. " (67-68)

In *Gods, Graves and Grandmother* there is also a repeated use of "and": "Phoolwati set up another stall just outside the temple which sold incense and marigold garlands and coconuts and little brass amulets which she ordered from Moradabad." (26) "The mourners came with garlands and incense sticks as offerings and soon air was sticky and sweet and turgid with the smells of sweet and marigold and incense." (75)

In *A Himalayan Love Story* we have the following examples: "Bareilly was hot and dusty and ugly and fascinating and I hoped against hope that a change of scene might improve things between us." (34) "They put me down unceremoniously, like a bundle, and settled themselves upon the rocks by the roadside to smile and smoke and gossip." (92-93) "Many years later, when I was still lonely and dreaming of Parvati, I had tossed and turned and clutched at my pillow, diagnosing, dissecting distorting the loves and hatreds of my youth." (137-38)

There is also a repeated use of "and" in the novel *The Book of Shadows:* "These are hardy and useful animals, clumsy, rough, and small, but sagacious, strong, and very sure-footed and docile." (48) "I felt somehow safe and secure and familiar, as though I was retreating or retiring to a place I already knew and recognized." (74)

In *Shakuntala: The Play of Memory* there are following examples of repeated use of "and": "They were showy and shiny and brilliant and made me feel both resentful and superior"

(145); "and so it was that Narangi had to sweep and swab and clean the offal of foreigners and Yavana outcastes to feed her sinful stomach." (157)

Imagery is used to signify all the objects and qualities of sense perception referred to in a work of literature, whether by literal description, by allusion, or in the vehicles of its similes and metaphors. Namita Gokhale is fond of imagery particularly animal imagery. She has sometimes drawn images from nature.

In *Paro: Dreams of Passion*, Paro's mental and physical condition, has been conveyed with the help of animal imagery. She was capable of bursting "into a massive horse-laugh." (27) At the sight of a male, her nostrils would get "slightly distended, like a mare's" (79) and she would very often respond "feverishly, obscenely, like a cat in heat." (80) She was thought to be "indeed a love-sick animal." (85) Even her laughter was not significantly different, "She grinned gleefully, like a satyr." (131)

An equally useful set of images are from the world of nature. The belly of Shambhu Nath Mishra was said to protrude obscenely "like a fat rotting pear." (79) When Paro heard about Lenin getting married, she was shattered and "tears were running down her cheeks like monsoon streams" (91) and after her accident she had "sort of shrivelled up after the accident, like an apple that has been stored too long." (163)

In *Gods, Graves and Grandmother*, the grandmother after Shambhu's murder was "still and sentinent as a hooded snake" (20) and "was motionless as a little mongoose." (20) Lila attended to grandmother's every need "with dog-like devotion." (65) Roxanne Madam's pair of glasses which she wore in the house were shaped differently, "They were elongated and elegant and made her look like a cat-woman." (87) After grandmother's death, Gudiya was taken to Roxanne's house; she was so hungry that the dinner sent to her room, she ate "with the ferocity of a starving animal." (92) The city of Delhi appeared to Gudiya as "a dying animal." (112)

In *A Himalayan Love Story* also Namita Gokhale has made use of imagery. The mad woman Parvati encountered in the forest cautioned her that she too would become mad and "clambered back on the tree with the lithe agility of young leopard." (15) After Lalit's death Parvati goes back to Wee Nooke where Raju and his wife came to meet her as they had come there for honeymoon, Raju's wife looked at Parvati "with pity and concern, as though, I were a sick animal or a stray dog." (50) Nainital had become crowded and people "swarmed like flies." (75) Young ghasiyarans who carried bundles of freshly scythed grass on their heads, walked "confident and sure-footed as the cows." (110) Mental illness ran in Kumaon "like a secret rivulet" (137) and Pushpendra blushes after meeting Mukul "like a beetroot" (142) are the nature imageries used.

In *The Book of Shadows* also, there is the use of animal imagery. To cite a few examples: the Botiya girl Lali would follow Cockerell with childish enthusiasm "like a playful puppy" (51) and Wolcott was awed by magician Crowley and "hung on him like a stray pup." (95) Gokhale has also made use of nature imagery to create an impact on readers. The cunning daayans said to Lahaniju "in voices as soft as the moonlight" (14) and Father Benedictus's "voluminous white beard which cascaded like a waterfall all the way to his knees." (130)

Shakuntala: The Play of Memory also abounds in abundant use of images. Shakuntala's mother had grown found of her after her brother had gone away; "as though, I was a pet parrot or a favourite calf." (27) Shakuntala's yearning for freedom is presented in the form of imagery, she wishes "Like the bird in the sacrificial altar, I too could soar across the sky." (55) For Shakuntala, Kamalini's figure "looked like a crane in flight" and her eyes "were like a serpent's" (57) or "she was like a high spirited stallion or an unfolding lotus bud." (65) Shakuntala thought that Guresvara, her brother was a scholar and a mendicant and he could "roam the world with the abandon of a wandering cloud." (68)

A symbol is a term used for something that represents something else. In principle, anything can symbolize anything else, temporarily or permanently especially something concrete or material used to represent something abstract or non-material, if an association can be formed between them. According to Rene Wellek and Austin Warren, "An image . . . if it persistently recurs both as presentation and representation it becomes a symbol."[9] F.A. Inamdar opines: "A symbol is a focus of relationship. It is hub of wheel around which plot, characters, setting move to evoke the central theme of the novel."[10]

Namita Gokhale has made an impressive use of symbolism in her fiction. According to Balram Sorot: "This device not only successfully conveys the changing patterns and variegated shades of life but also provides the novels with multiple and deeper meanings. Besides the characters who represent certain ideas and ideals, there are some situations, gestures, plants, songs and animals that suggest something beyond their literal meanings."[11]

The title of the novel *Paro: Dreams of Passion* is symbolic because the novel deals with the frank delineation of human beings proclivity to those passions, both elemental and transitory, to which human mind and flesh have been heir from times immemorial. Paro was all for frank enjoyment of sensual passions. She would wrap a man "as completely as a banana skin." (155) She becomes the "symbol of and prototype of emancipation and individuality." (48) The relationship of Paro and Priya, at one level, symbolizes the envy and hatred which a plain—looking girl unconsciously and universally has, for a girl who possesses a natural charm and vivacity. The present given by Paro to Priya of a screaming woman which ultimately results in Priya's abortion symbolizes Paro's hatred and jealousy at seeing her happiness. Priya's habit of fantasizing as Paro, symbolizes a middle class girls desire to rise above her middle class surroundings. Priya's choice of Suresh on the basis of his car was also the attempt to acquire status.

Gods, Graves and Grandmother abounds in symbols. The temple symbolizes the faith of people in religious things. Ammi's resourcefulness was indicated when she builds up a temple from a marble slab and rocks stolen from neighbourhood rockery which also symbolizes her firm faith in her own ability. Lila's devotion to Ammi, symbolizes idol worship. Then we have Gudiya changing her name to Pooja Abhimanyu Singh, symbolizing her desire to assert her adulthood. The peepal tree talking to Gudiya and at times scolding and showing her displeasure by moving her leaves when Gudiya steals a coin symbolizes Gudiya's desire for a companion in her lonely life. Since grandmother becomes indifferent to her, she looks up to peepal tree as a presence in her life. The dusty and desolate Delhi city with its crowd symbolizes monstrous growth which is degrading and devastating. The banana tree having miraculous appearance of ripe yellow bananas overnight is the symbol of miracles taking place in human life.

In *A Himalayan Love Story*, Parvati was fond of collecting pine cones much to the annoyance of her mother. When asked by her mother what she would do with them, her reply that she would build a palace is symbolic of her desire to become rich. Mukul's devotion to Hiranand Headmaster symbolizes a void created in his life due to his father's death. When he comes to Nainital after receiving Hiranand Headmaster's letter is a symbol of an NRI's desire to do something for his people.

The painting and re-painting of the nails with dark colours by Rachita in *The Book of Shadows*, is a symbol of her struggle for sanity and existence. Lohaniju never leaves the house and always names the dog of the house "Lady" is symbolic of his devotion to the house. The hill house where Rachita goes to stay after acid attack symbolizes love and care. Anand's suicide is symbolic of lack of understanding, communication, faith and perseverance towards his relationship with Rachita. Dona Rosa's relationship with Wolcott and other men visiting the house symbolizes lust. The Himalaya's symbolize persistence and permanence and the soothing effect of nature on Rachita's troubled mind. It is an inspiration and strength for her struggle for existence.

In *Shakuntala: The Play of Memory* river Ganga symbolizes life. She carries within her the secrets of past, present and future. The river flowing through the mountain symbolizes purity and innocence but when she comes to the plain, she symbolizes pollution and degradation. The star of Arundhati is the symbol of fidelity. Shakuntala's going with Nearchus leaving her husband symbolizes her desire for knowledge on one hand and on the other unfaithfulness and infidelity.

Irony in rhetoric means words with an implication opposite to their usual meaning. Ironic comment may be humorous or mildly sarcastic. In general usage it is incongruity between what is expected and what happens and an outcome that displays such incongruity.

Namita Gokhale has used irony effectively to throw an illuminating light upon some peculiar aspects of her characters or exemplify the unreality or absurdity of certain situations. In *Paro: Dreams of Passion*, Gokhale uses irony to bring out the character traits of Paro. Rape is considered to be the most humiliating, disgracing, traumatizing thing affecting the psyche and entire life of the victim. Paro was raped by her art teacher but this event does not affect Paro the way it should have, instead she confesses to Priya that she loved every moment of it.

Another incident of irony is found when Priya tells that her mother was suffering from cough and her brother, who was studying medicine was unconcerned about her condition. The verbal irony is revealed through the utterances of Paro, who was prevented from going to Lenin's wedding. Although she wanted to go yet she pretended that she would look out of place in the wedding at Ramnagar, a small town. She says: "Don't be silly, yaar. The country hicks will stare at me like somebody from a zoo. Let Priya go and represent all of us," she said flippantly." (97-98)

Irony is also evident in *Gods, Graves and Grandmother*. Gudiya and her grandmother established a temple although they were Muslims. They made use of the resources available and people started visiting the temple religiously. Gudiya tells: "In the evening we lit an earthen lamp at the shrine and performed aarti. Shambhu of the tea stall produced a large luminous conch shell from which he coaxed an awesome and angry wail. Two strangers stopped by on their way home from office. They clapped and kept time as grandmother clanged the brass bell that had magically materialized and now hung like some mystical fruit from the branches of the peepal tree. I was still a stranger to the paraphernalia of religion, brought up as I had been ignorant of God or Divinity, and I puzzled to make sense of the unfamiliar tableau as the flickering lamp cast new shadows on my grandmother's trusted face." (2-3)

Another instance of irony is fond when Pandit Kailash Shastry predicts Gudiya's future. He predicts not only wealth, fortune, position which are ordinary things but the real blessings of the almighty like wisdom, knowledge, good name and fame. But we find that none of these things happen in Gudiya's life. He told Ammi: "The lines on Gudiya's forehead," he said, "these lines are to be seen in one in a million faces. Mukkadar ki Sikandar—Gudiya's destiny awaits her. No, not only wealth, fortune, position for these are ordinary things, but wisdom, knowledge, goodname fame—the real blessings of the Almighty." (65)

The death scene of Sundar Pahalwan is also described ironically. Sundar being an anti-social element was shot dead by his enemies. The Police arrived at the scene without being informed. They were unsympathetic towards the grieving widow, Phoolwati. Gudiya tells us: "When the Police arrived they were not much gentler. They interrogated Phoolwati mercilessly and settled themselves on her plush new sofas like an occupying force. A press photographer also arrived, and he took a picture of the grieving widow. The policemen kept demanding tea and there was nobody to make it but me." (235)

In *A Himalayan Love Story* also Namita Gokhale has made use of irony to highlight the incongruities of life. Parvati tells us that in Jeolikote almost everybody owned a cow and they also deserved to have one. Her mother thought of a number of schemes to raise money but neither worked. Then they grew corn behind their shop but there was excessive harvest of corn that year and they had to eat corn every day. They could not collect money to buy a cow but instead had problem disposing the corn: "We cleared a patch of land behind the shop, and raised a splendid harvest of corn. But there was a surfeit of corn that year, and after my mother had subcontracted with the chai-wala, disaster struck. The chai-wala decamped to Kathgodam on a drunken binge, where he fell off the railway platform onto the tracks and was mashed to pulp by an incoming train from Lucknow. Since his wife was not as generous as he had been, even our supplies of free milk dried up. Moreover, we were stuck with vast quantities of corn every day, and still there was plenty left over, which my mother hung from the kitchen rafters for the winter months." (8-9)

Then they tried to take up bee-keeping to earn enough money to buy a cow. They got the pamphlets from the bee-keeping institute and Parvati read them out to her mother who was satisfied that, Parvati's education was being put to some use. She even thought that Parvati would become a teacher someday. But their attempts to earn extra money turned out to be unsuccessful: "We abandoned the idea. We never made the extra money to afford a cow." (11)

Gokhale has used irony effectively to show the efforts made by Parvati to raise money for Lalit's treatment of T.B. Relatives were requested for some loans, Lalit also wrote a letter to his boss, Parvati wrote letters to Masterji and Mukul. But before financial help arrived, Lalit had died: "My father-in-law, the post master, tried to get a loan from some relatives. Lalit wrote a letter to his boss in the factory. We received a reply saying that the management was 'considering' the request. I wrote a letter to Masterji and another to Mukul Nainwal, asking for help. But before I could post either of them, Lalit had died." (47)

Rachita in *The Book of Shadows* sometimes felt that she should return to the city and her job. But it is an irony that isolation had made her incapable of facing the world: "Perhaps it is time for me to leave, to return to the city, to my job. But I don't know if I can ever return, loneliness feeds on isolation until one day you realize you just can't face anything any more." (61)

It was again an irony that Rachita who was not comfortable with Hindi, had to read Mahadevi Verma's poems to spend her time in that lonely house: "I'm not comfortable with Hindi, with the Devnagari script, and yet I am compelled to read these poems. I am drawn to them as a moth to the candle, to use the rather hyperbolic language and metaphor of Mahadevi Verma herself." (72)

In *Shakuntala: The Play of Memory*, there are also instances of irony. On their wedding night, Shakuntala's husband, Srijan, took her to the courtyard, behind the house and showed her the star of Arundhati. He told her: "Beyond the tree, above the mountain, you can see the star of Arundhati. She is the purest of wives, the emblem of fidelity. As you see that star by my guidance, so I shall guide you in our life together towards the vision of right and wrong." (42)

But, Shakuntala pretends that she had not seen the star. It is ironical that her husband was expecting a pure wife but Shakuntala runs away with Nearchus. The second ironical situation is found when Shakuntala reminds herself that she was the wife Srijan, the Mahasamant and she should conduct herself accordingly but she deserts her home and family for the company of a Greek horse merchant and acquires a name Yaduri—the fallen woman. When she runs away with Nearchus she forgets the Arundhati star—the emblem of fidelity and so also that she was the wife of a Mahasamant.

Another ironical situation is found when Shakuntala, who was hungry for knowledge and experience, reaches Kashi, the city of her imagination along with Nearchus but it is ironical that she could not live in main city of Kashi. She had to live on the other side of the river, the part which was meant for the foreigners so that Kashi remains pure: "As for this city where I witness my ruination, this is not the dwelling of the twice—born that my brother told me about in that other lifetime. It is the quarter of the Yavanas, unfinished men without a home who are to be kept away from the holy city. And so am I." (16)

Namita Gokhale is also gifted with rich sense of humour. She may occasionally, tinge the serious flowing narrative with a tone of lightness, thus relieving the reader of the looming tragedy, and making him laugh at the incongruities of the situations or characters.

In *Paro: Dreams of Passion* Priya's adventurous visit to the parlour before going to Paro and B.R.'s wedding reception is humorously presented by Priya: "The hairdresser's assistant could, with unerring instinct, smell out my somewhat dubious social status and did his best to knot the curlers and nets into the most uncomfortable configuration possible. When I emerged from the cocoon of the dryer I had not, to my intense disappointment, turned into any butterfly. The assistant presented the mirror with a malicious flourish, and I found myself face-to-face with a stranger, and a decidedly unattractive stranger at that." (7)

Priya had heard about Paro's beauty. She also wanted to look good. But after coming out of the parlour she could not recognize herself. Then the readers are amused to read about Priya's mother telling her about the marriage offer: "Priya, Priya beti, ek khushkhabari hai." she said theatrically. Then predictably, she burst into unabashed sobs; I sat, perplexed, until her sobs subsided. Presently she began tenderly to stroke my hair. 'Kitni sundar dulhan banegi,' she said, holding my chin in her work-hardened hands and looking long and tenderly into my eyes until I winced with pain." (19)

The entire scene appears to have come out straight from a movie as Priya always referred to her mother as filmi mother. Priya also tells us that Suresh was a very friendly man and offered himself to his friends as a joker: "Suresh affected a bluff good humour, and would offer himself quite without rancour as joker, buffoon and spittoon to his social and economic superiors." (24)

The woman who became the part of the group formed by Suresh and Priya looked like Priya or worse. They would meet at get togethers, drink beer or whisky, cigarette smoke and ghazals. Then they would go home but there was no camaraderie only competitiveness. This is again a humorous situation. Then we have Mary informing Priya about B.R. through a letter. It is a fine piece of humour. She writes: "The big boss is still sighted around Bombay sometimes, hunting for all kinds of goodies to eat . . . but wifey number two is no longer in the kitchen not that she ever was, ha ha !" (119)

Her letter was full of digestive metaphors. She called Priya's heart "sweet chocolate heart" and told her that her "figure has become like Tun Tun with my own cooking, and as Robert is still as trim as ever, I have to be very careful to make sure that the way to his heart remains through his stomach." (119)

Gods, Graves and Grandmother is also not without humour. In fact Gokhale's humour has been often mentioned as surreal humour. She looks for humour in all situations, often in serious moments. Soon after founding the rudimentary temple, the grandmother "prostrated herself before the pebbles and the marigolds on the green marble slab, lay down so still and silent and for so long that" Gudiya thought "I was afraid she might be dead or in a coma." (2) Gudiya whispered in her ear, "Are you all right, Ammi?" (2) Shambhu coaxed from his large luminous conch-shell "an awesome and angry wail." (2) Soon after the founding of the temple, Gudiya saw "A man in a helmet, clutching a briefcase in his folded hand, was standing beneath the peepal tree, his head bowed in prayer." (3) The young woman Magoo succumbed to Shambhu's charms and they were always "smiling into each other's eyes, although Shambhu of course had only one." (17)

Phoolwati suffered from gas problem which has been described with ridiculous and exaggerated details: "Phoolwati suffered intensely from 'gas.' She would contort her substantial figure to improbable postures to ease its passage, coax it out through burp or belch. But an eternal spring of 'vayu' seemed to reside in her innards, and her life became an increasing torrent of internal turmoil." (56)

On being taken to task she would reply "bhoga is the most difficult part of yoga." (56) Panditji was requested to hold the discourses in lieu of the evening bhajans—"soon his stern voice began to blast the evenings, amplified by the crackling mike, scaring away the crows, not to speak of the devotees." (120-21)

While sermonizing angrily, Panditji "sighed philosophically, eyeing the day's takings." (122) When Lila addresses the devotees in absence of Phoolwati, she talked about the late Mataji's important message to her devotees—that Mataji had described 'swarga' to her: "She says it is a very nice place; the weather is very pleasant, not hot and dusty like our Delhi. The people are all very beautiful, tall and fair and graceful, rather like our Gudiya. The air is clear and the food is good, although of course they don't need to eat anything there. It's only for the taste, if you get what I mean, sometimes a mango, sometimes a mithai." (142)

The novel *A Himalayan Love Story* also has humour. We are told by Parvati about Lalit's family waiting for a good news although there were many children in the family: "Everybody in Lalit's family was waiting for some 'good news': the surfeit of nieces and nephews that swarmed about their Nainital home had evidently not satisfied my in-laws desire for progeny." (39)

When Raju found Parvati sleeping in the kitchen along with rats and vermin, instead of being surprised he asked her grinning "So that's how the land lies, is it?" he grinned. "Is this a lover's quarrel or has my respected brother's hatred of the fair sex finally asserted itself." (40)

Then we have the information about strawberries being sold to the tourists who come to Jeolikote: "These were sold in cane baskets to the summer tourists, cunningly disguised in weight and worth by the heap of mulberry leaves on which they were artfully spread out." (3-4)

We are told that Hiranand Headmaster was called 'Masterji' in Jeolikote and was an important man in Nainital. Parvati's mother was always importuned with letters of reference for admission to his school and requests for waiver of fees etc, all of which she gracefully accepted but never showed him. Masterji had thus achieved a quite underserved reputation in Jeolikote for being 'unhelpful,' still "the hopeful letters and introductions did not cease." (6)

In *The Book of Shadows* also, there are instances of humour. For brevity few are cited. Lohaniju, the caretaker of the house, does not leave the house; we are told by Rachita: "Lohaniju loves the house, he has lived here all his life. He has never been to Nainital, never been to Almora. The furthest he has ever ventured from the house is to Ranikhet market, where he goes once a week for the shopping and to pick up the mail." (11)

The frequent powercuts are also presented in humorous words, "The electricity has failed, it often does in the evenings." (BS, 23-24) Humour arises from the fact that electric lights are needed only when it is dark. The electric current is available during day when it is not needed. One needs light to get rid of darkness. Humour arises because lights are there when not needed and not there when needed.

Shakuntala: The Play of Memory also has humour. After Shakuntala's brother went to hermitage, Shakuntala was discovered by her mother as if she did not exist before: "The year that Govinda went to the hermitage, Mother, to my great delight, decided to take me to the fair with her. It was as if she had discovered me, now that the sun had departed and her eyes, were not blinded by his dazzle." (12)

Shakuntala's brother returns from his hermitage since the great Rishi who taught him, was too quick tempered and expected his students to do well. Her mother found another teacher to teach him grammar and religious texts which he did religiously. Shakuntala tells: "All morning my brother would sit with his tutor monotonously rehearsing the ritual pada-patha of the Krama-patha, and the grammar of the jnana-patha, struggling with the perpetuation of learning which is the true task of the high-born mind." (16)

Shakuntala was surprised and amused when Nearchus told her about the horse trading. He told that horses were sold in the royal courts and their hair was used as braids of women: "He told me of wild horses twice the size of normal horses that were sought for their tails, fine as a woman's hair. Elegant ladies in the great cities made coiffures and braids of them, intertwining them with their own natural hair. Horse hair on women!" (134)

When the cleaning woman Narangi asks Shakuntala her name she replied, "Shakuntala" but further added that the

Yavana, "knows me only as Yaduri." (3) Narangi reflects on the name as it meant a fallen woman and gives an amusing explanation: "What's in a name?" she said. Further she informs Shakuntala, "When I was a child, my mother had named me Rajrani! Now, do I look in the least like queen or princess to you? Maharani of the slop buckets! I changed my name to Narangi to please myself." (153)

Thus the detailed study of the narrative technique used by Namita Gokhale reveals her as a master artist, narrating her stories interestingly by giving lively description and handling her prose dexterously. She has experimented with language to bring about the desired effect and impact. To keep in touch with her Indian roots, she has liberally used Indian words and Indian situations. The use of imagery, symbolism and humour and the sincerity of purpose further enhance the appeal of her fiction which though dealing with varied Indian life, has a wider and universal significance.

The mode of expression adopted by Gokhale is the first-person narrative with recurrent use of flash-backs. She uses this technique in all her novels. Priya, Gudiya, Parvati, Mukul, Rachita, William Cockerell, Ghost and Shakuntala are the characters narrating their stories and recollecting the past events. Indian words are abundantly used in her novels without translating them into English to mark the individuality as well as the Indianness of the character who use them. Collective nouns are used by her to give exact details of the quantity.

The figures of speech like similes, metaphors, personification, alliterations and repetition are remarkably used to stress her point of view. An impressive use of symbolism is made to convey the deeper meaning. Gokhale's novels are scattered with instances of imagery. Nature as well as zoological images are widely used. The comparison gives the reader an insight into the author's purpose of using it.

Among various stylistic devices that Gokhale employs in her fiction are, irony and humour. She uses irony effectively to bring forth either the peculiarities of her characters or exemplify the absurdities or unrealities of certain situations. Gokhale is also gifted with rich sense of humour which is amply displayed when she describes a character or situation.

NOTES

1. R. K. Dhawan, "Preface," *Explorations in Modern English Fiction*. New Delhi: Bahri, 1992, p. 1
2. Paul Varghese, Qtd. Somerset Maugham, *Literary Criticism—A Workbook*. Madras: Macmillan India, 1981, p. 80.
3. *Ibid*., 80.
4. Anne Sherril and Paula Robertson Rose. *Four Elements: A Creative Approach to the Short Story*. New York: Holt, Rinehart and Winston, 1975, p. 78.
5. Meenakshi Mukherjee, Qtd. "An Area of Brightness," *The Week*. 26 July 1996, p. 4.
6. Raja Rao, "Foreword," Kanthapura. London: George Allen and Unwin, 1968.
7. Meenakshi Mukherjee, "The Problem of Style," *The Twice-Born Fiction*. New Delhi: Arnold Heinemann, 1971, p. 170.
8. R.S. Pathak, "Indianization of English: Language and Literature," *Indianization of English Language and Literature*, ed. R.S. Pathak, New Delhi: Bahri, 1994.
9. Rene Wellek and Austin Warren, *Theory of Literature*. London: Penguin, 1949.
10. F.A. Inamdar, "Image and Symbol Pattern in Kamala Markandaya's Novels," *Indian Writing in English*, Vol. 1, New Delhi: Atlantic, 1998.
11. Balram Sorot, "Craftsmanship," *The Novels of Bhabani Bhattacharya*. New Delhi: Prestige, 1991.

Memorable Creations

It is an uphill task for a novelist to create memorable characters who will linger in the memory of the readers long after the novel has been read. The writers take inspiration and ideas from the people they come across from all walks of life. Society provides them with the raw material needed to produce the final product. The observations and the experiences of the writer are woven into a fine blend to create characters which become memorable.

Indian women novelists are aware of the treatment meted out to women by society. They are highly conscious about women's liberation movement. In their novels they have portrayed women and their stories from the viewpoint of the injustice suffered by them. These novels have a feminist approach. Women as central characters are depicted in these novels. They rebel against the existing social set-up. They are no more shown to be a submissive, suffering, and sacrificing lot. Rebellion being not an easy process demands determination, will and courage to stand by the cause and face the consequences, come what may. The women characters in the novels of Indian women novelists have often paid the price of their rebellion rather than submitting or suffocating.

The awareness of individual needs of women like self-assertion, self-fulfillment and self-identity by the writers have resulted in the novels having themes of alienation, communication gap, identity crisis, broken relationships and quest for freedom. Women in the novels of Nayantara Sahgal are liberal and unconventional. Ruth Prawer Jhabvala's women do not go against traditions out of any firm conviction but they appear modern. Shashi Deshpande's women are educated, self-conscious and sensitive. Necessity is the cause for their revolt against rigid social and familial set-up. Kamala Markandaya has presented mixed spectrum of heroines who do not lose identity and mental strength while conforming to the social set-up. Anita Desai's women are not only liberated but they go much beyond to the region of psychological and philosophical depths. Shobha De through her characters has hit hard against the prevailing norms.

Namita Gokhale in her novels has presented a plethora of characters. Women are the central figures of her novels. She has depicted their likes, dislikes, aspirations, desires, quest for freedom and search for identity. Her characters belong to upper middle-class, middle-class, metropolitan slums and even ancient traditional class. Women in her novels assert themselves. They have their own priorities. Bodily needs are not neglected. Women characters have the full appetite for life and the capacity to face the world boldly. Male characters are also dealt with but much emphasis is laid on the portrayal of women characters, thus giving men the secondary status. Let us examine various characters portrayed by her in her five novels.

Namita Gokhale in *Paro: Dreams of Passion* presents the story of Paro, the seductress and Priya, the narrator. Paro is the central character who is the only child. She spends her whole life in the boarding school in the hills where she had a crush on Marcus, her art master who rapes her. She is eventually expelled from the school. This incident probably lays the foundation for her sexual journey and makes her aware of her physical assets. She makes an attempt to break the shackles of conventions and attains emancipation. As Sharad Shrivastav opines: "For, in this process a woman has first to liberate herself from her middle-class pseudo-morality in order to break herself free from male-dominance."[1]

Priya, the narrator of Paro's story and her own informs us at the very beginning of the novel how Paro broke the conventions when she made an appearance at her own wedding-reception. She marries B.R., the sewing machine industrialist, whom she meets in college and who falls for her "like a ton of bricks." (32) Her appearance is shocking to middle-class sensibility of Priya and even to Paro's parents. Priya tells us: "Her audacity and confidence took my breath away. This was not how brides behaved in my world. All the brides I had ever encountered kept their heads—which were so perilously downcast as to appear anatomically endangered—well-covered with their sari pallavs. But she stood proud and straight, and led the way, with B.R. and her parents trailing after her: "She circulated through the room with an assured catlike grace. One mehndied hand carelessly held on to, horror of horrors, a glass of gin! The other was graciously bestowed on B. R., who followed in her wake, a slightly glazed look in his fine eyes." (10-11)

Paro's behaviour towards her father-in-law was also unconventional. Her audacity and self-confidence took Priya's breath away: "Hi, Daddiji," she said throatily planting a kiss smack on Rai Bahadur's forehead—she had to bend over slightly to reach him. (10)

For her marriage was also not a permanent thing. In one of the conversations with Priya, she expresses her opinions about marriage in one sentence: "I always knew it [marriage] sounded too good to last. And it didn't." (32) After a short marital stint with B.R., she starts living in open adulterous relationship with Bucky Bhandpur, test cricketer and scion of a princely family. "She liberated herself from marriage and convention" (26). Priya describes Paro's new role as a woman who has raised herself above liberation or emancipation. She observes: "Life has not tired her" also "she is undiminished." (26) Paro's relationship with 'Bucky' Bhandpur does not last long. She leaves him and thus becomes a liberated woman who has "left a husband and a lover" and has "a small son of ambiguous parentage." (26) Thus she breaks the conventions and dares to have a child whose father is unknown. Her revolt against the social and moral codes acts as a means to create a place for her in the society. As pointed out by Kuldeep Kumar and Gajendra Kumar: "Paro's outgoing nature helped her to become a social celebrity very soon. She came out of the areas which were allotted to women and succeeded in making a place for her in male-dominated society. Paro came out of the traditional image of a woman, who was forced to remain inside the house where she was expected to do nothing else than household chores, child-bearing and child-rearing."[2]

Next man to enter her life was Priya's husband, Suresh. At this time Paro was facing a lot of legal problems. Suresh's intention was to use her contacts for his own gain but actually he too was attracted towards Paro, who started visiting Priya's house regularly and on one such occasion she narrated the incident of her school with tears in her eyes. She was raped by her art master Marcus during Dussehra vacations: "He raped me in a grove of pine trees," she said, tears in her eyes. "He sodomised me in the woods behind the chapel." (29-30)

She was expelled from the school when found with the art master in her room. Though she was the victim of the lust of a male, yet as she herself confesses: "Funny thing is that I wasn't raped, I loved every moment of it." (32) As Priya points out, she was not ashamed of her sexual encounters: "She did not perceive the shame or furtiveness of sex. She talked of mating her bitch and the complexities of her own sexual life with the same directness and with the same degree of involvement." (33)

Later on she develops relationship with a young boy called Avinendra, the son of the Minister of State for Industry. Priya affectionately called him Lenin for his Marxist leanings and appearance. He considered Paro to be a free woman, a real individual and therefore he loved her intensely. Once in a hotel, while they were dining, he proclaims: "'Now this lady . . .' he would say, looking at Paro with an intensity which I thought was almost manic, 'is a real individual. She has the courage of her convictions. She is not a kept woman; she is free. That is why I love her.'" (47)

Avinendra was totally besotted by Paro but it was shocking for his parents to find their son in the company of that kind of woman. He was completely dependent upon her emotionally. Priya wondered whether it was a mother-fixation. Paro wanted to marry him but could not as in one of their fights Lenin had called her a whore. She also establishes relationship with Shambhu Nath Mishra, a congress man who, according to Priya, was the ugliest man: "He was black as the night, black as the carpet, and his belly protruded obscenely from his chest, like a fat rotting pear. All this was balanced on the thinnest, spindliest legs possible. An immaculately starched white khadi topi nestled on his thick, suspiciously black hair." (79)

Her affair with Mishraji became one of the hottest scandals. Their affair was much talked about in the Delhi's ostentatious social circuit. The whole situation also puzzled Priya who was stunned by Paro's absolute emotional surrender: "I could not understand the situation. I could well ascribe the worst possible motives to her, and suspect her of having a liaison with such an influential figure for all the implicit and unsubtle gains she could derive from her position as his mistress. What left me totally stunned was her absolute and unconditional emotional surrender." (81-82)

Soon, Mishraji started becoming tired of such "smothering devotion." The more he avoided her, the more she would thrust herself upon him. On being asked by Suresh as to why she was so much after that old man, she replied honestly: "He is so ugly, so repulsive that he makes me feel beautiful." (84)

She even managed to go with him to America for a World Conference but her passion was spent when she returned and she got rid of him from her life. Once again she went back to 'Bucky' Bhandpur for a short while.

The last man in her life is the Greek film-maker, Loukas Leoros, who is a professed homosexual. She marries him and as the article in the magazine described, it was, "A marriage of true minds." (148) Priya knew that Paro was capable of doing daring and unpredictable things. Loukas had come to India to do a documentary and found a universal mother in form of Paro: 'He came to India to document on film the female anima, the compelling Lilith like forces of Life and femininity, what we Hindu call Maya. After a week's whirlwind romance, he has plunged headlong into his first matrimonial adventure. But his bride, Paro, is already a veteran of two marriages. Her ex-husband, Raja Birendra Singh of the erstwhile state of Bhandpur, was in fact the best man at the wedding. "I knew when I met her," Leoros says, "that I had at last met my mother—for Paro is the universal mother."' (148)

As Subhash Chandra points out: "Paro's sexual encounters with men become both a means of asserting the power of her femaleness and an exercise in defining herself. It seems that she is driven by a subconscious urge to be herself, to discard the constraints that a patriarchal cultural set-up imposes on woman to conform to the image constructed and perpetuated by the male."[3]

Paro was not dependent on anyone as she herself declared: "I am myself, and no one else, I depend on nobody. I am my own person." (48) Paro was also a self-centred person. Whenever she met Priya, she would only talk about herself and would never bother to ask about Priya: "She would come and sit for hours on end. She would talk on, compulsively, about herself, always herself. Compulsively, I would listen. She never asked me anything about myself and I in turn never ventured to tell." (29)

Priya also observed that Paro loved her body and cried like a baby if she was physically hurt. She was not concerned about her son and the impact of her behaviour on him. This was evident when Shambhu Nath Mishra came to Paro's barsati or when Paro went out with him. Junior, her son would watch everything horrified, just like children at a massacre, helpless and immobilized. She always told Lenin to look after Junior whenever the need arose. She was so engrossed in her own self that she did not fulfill her motherly responsibilities. Paro loved self-dramatization and Priya sometimes wondered what she must be doing when she was alone: "Her fatal flaw was vanity. She loved self-dramatization. I sometimes wondered what she would be like alone in an empty room; whether she would simply go limp and collapse, or posture and practise for her next encounter." (33)

Her self-dramatization always had a desired impact on men. Paro wanted to marry Lenin but he saw her whoring. They had a massive fight: she was shrieking because Lenin had called her a whore. Everyone was horrified at the sight of her getting quite filmi. Her self-dramatization had a desired effect on Lenin: "Lenin was watching in horror and I could see that the tide of his emotions had changed, and that the magnetism of her moonlike body held him in as complete a thrall as ever before. He bent down and began feverishly to kiss her feet; she gave him a hard kick on his face, then on his groin." (55)

Paro then lay on the bed, motionless. Blood dripped from her wrists to little puddles down the floor. She had slashed her wrists with Priya's ladies shaving razor but she survived. After this unsuccessful suicide attempt, her hold over Lenin became even stronger. She used her tactical advantage shamelessly and relentlessly and became an absolute tyrant for she knew how to utilize her beauty for her own gains. As she herself clarified when Priya calls it an emotional blackmail: ""Oh, no!" she replied. "It's part of being a Beautiful Woman. It's a full-time occupation. And much harder work than it seems. But"—nodding sagely—"it has its rewards, I confess."' (62)

Priya thought her to be a faddist at heart and considered her short-lived enthusiasm as almost a primitive exhibitionism. She made everyone follow what she did. She joined yoga classes which she made Lenin join along with her. She would insist Lenin to wake up early in the morning and drive her down to India Gate lawns, where they had to undergo all kinds of gruesome physical exercises in public. She would then display her skills to all and sundry irrespective of suitability of the occasion. At a chic cocktail party she shocked everyone by standing on her head for a minute: "Suddenly I found Paro throwing down her pallav and wrapping it around her waist, lungi style, and before I could even figure out what was happening, she was on the grass, sandals kicked off, and two long beautiful white legs pointing like cranes to the night sky. She stood like that, on her head, for over a minute." (64) Then there were her salad-days. She made everyone suffer for her new-found passion for green and for things uncooked. She declared that cooking was unhealthy, unnatural and unhygienic. She called Priya and her husband for salad lunch every Sunday.

Priya instinctively understood Paro's potential for destruction and did her best to keep away from her. Incapable of knowing the meaning of happiness or how to remain happy, Paro destroyed Priya's innocent happiness on conception. When Priya threw a small birthday party for Suresh, Paro was also invited against the wishes of Priya. Paro gave a birthday present to Suresh which was a metal and bronze statue of a screaming woman with a staring totemic sort of owl in the foreground. There was terror in the woman's eyes. This modern art-piece horrified Priya and became the cause for her miscarriage.

Paro had a desire to know herself for which she took to theatre acting. She played the role of Clytemnestra in *Aeschylus*, the trilogy. She told Priya that she identified herself with Clytemnestra because she was also very enigmatic like her: "So I went for a few auditions, and I found that I really identified, like, with this woman. I sort of empathize, you know, all the contradictions in my own life. This Clytemnestra is a passionate and strong woman, with this creepy husband. So she kills him. So her son kills her." (110-11)

But this play-acting was short-lived. Paro exhibited suicidal tendency. She attempted suicide thrice, of which the last one proved to be fatal. She first attempted suicide when she found B.R. with a neighbour's daughter. The second attempt she makes when Lenin calls her a whore. The third attempt turned out to be fatal when at the party hosted by her to celebrate her recovery from an accident, Paro slashed her wrists with a fruit knife when everybody was on a high during a party. Priya could read an immense dejection on her face as if she had realized the futility of her struggle.

Paro's suicide has been variously interpreted by the critics. Sharad Shrivastav opines: "Paro who has successfully handled all her amorous adventures, is quick to realize that without her beauty and physical charm she would no longer continue to have her sway over men. Towards the end of the novel, Paro throws a party to celebrate her recovery after the 'accident.' The realization that her 'charm' is no longer on her side forces her to slash her wrists and puts an end to this meaningless sex adventure spree."[4]

R.S. Pathak considers Paro to be the product of her circumstances. He says: "Paro tried to take life in her stride but was caught unawares. Disillusioned and disgusted with her life, she put an end to it and thus met with the fate reserved for all egocentric sensualists."[5]

Thus, Paro's struggle for freedom and self-assertion ended in her death. Perhaps she was tired with the life she had chosen to lead in future. Priya who is the narrator of *Paro: Dreams of Passion* has a fascination for Paro. She writes about Paro and B.R. because she sees herself in Paro. She was deeply hurt as Paro snatches away B.R. with whom Priya had a sexual liaison.

Priya was the secretary of B.R. All the girls in the office including Priya were madly in love with him and all of them hated Paro. She became an obsession for Priya who started imitating her: "I would find myself mouthing her words; phrases that were not mine would spell unsuspecting from my lips; gestures that were hers would enact themselves in involuntary mime. For example, I too would throw back my head in a deep throaty laugh, and my eyes would narrow in a pale shadow of her piercing gaze." (13)

Priya was so obsessed by Paro that she started imagining herself to be Paro. She tried to follow Paro and started smoking, visiting beauty parlours and wore modern dresses. But Suresh, Priya's husband, objected to it as he wanted Priya to be a typical Indian woman wearing only sarees. Priya's house-keeping after marriage to Suresh was also an act of imitating Paro and her home with B.R.: "I filled the balcony of the first-floor flat with a profusion of potted plants, which I tended with an almost religious fervour. I would spend the afternoons there sipping at my tea and leafing through magazines." (21)

Priya even stitched tea-cloths and embroidered them for her trousseau as she saw in Paro's house. During her sleep, Paro's endearments meant for B.R. would arise unbidden to her lips. She was convinced that her child was conceived after so many years of sterility, at a moment when she was pretending to be Paro. Sharad Shrivastav comments on Priya's attitude: "Paro represents the dreams of passion and social glitter and emancipation that Priya can never realize. Yet within the humble surroundings of her middle-class existence, Priya does make efforts to emancipate herself socially and morally."[6]

Priya was ashamed of her middle-class atmosphere and she secretly vowed to come out of this atmosphere. She was aware of the fact that her asthmatic mother and a phlegmatic brother can only be a hindrance in her dreaming. So, she decided to materialize her 'dreams of passion' by acquiring a husband having some status. Hence, when she was shown the photograph of Suresh leaning against a standard Herald car, she gave her consent for marriage. Suresh was her distant relative, he was a lawyer in Delhi and came from a prosperous and decent family. As she confesses, the car decided for her to get married to Suresh. Like Paro, Priya also realised quite early that men are to be used for women's personal situations. In the middle-class social set-up to which Priya belonged, unmarried girls were supposed to be virgins but Priya had lost her virginity before her marriage. Her husband was unable to notice the fact. She admits: "My marriage was a middle-class one, much as any other. We did not have many relatives, and so it was uneventful, even a little boring. My husband was a virgin, and did not seem to notice that I was not." (20)

During the early years of her married life with Suresh, Priya attempted to become a society lady but was discouraged by Suresh. He tolerated her going to parlour for a hair cut but disapproved her smoking or wearing anything but sarees. She came back to her Indian image but soon realized that Suresh was the weapon by which she could meet her personal ends. She was honest to confess and was successful in her endeavour: "I realised that my only weapon in an indifferent world was Suresh, and I decided to groom him patiently until my ministrations bore dividends. We short-listed the thirty or so people in the legal and allied professions who could be useful to us, and along with smattering of friends (for Suresh was a very friendly man, a natural extrovert), started hosting regular informal get-togethers at home." (24)

This intensive programme of cultivation became successful and they formed a group of smart young people who put on a brave front of gaiety and good times. Every weekend there would be a get-together somewhere and over beer or whisky, cigarette smoke and ghazals, they would try to keep themselves updated with the changing world. Yet, they were not bound together by camaraderie but by an intense competitiveness.

Priya's attraction for B.R. continued even after her marriage to Suresh. She got an opportunity to meet B.R. when she went to Bombay. She would meet B.R. almost every evening and have candle-light dinner. They would make love in anonymous hotel rooms. It was a revival of dream for her and she did not want to let go those moments. She confesses: "It was a second youth, a middle-aged revival of dreams. I had indeed never ever dreamt of such passion, and I kept delaying the inevitable return to Delhi and Suresh's clumsy hateful arms." (39)

Although those were the happiest days in Priya's life, she had to return to Delhi. At home Suresh told Priya hesitatingly that during her absence he had heard some gossip about her and B.R. But he also assured her that he had absolute faith in her. However, he felt that it was not good for women from good families to be talked about. Priya feigned surprise and refused to have any such relationship with B.R. Rashmi Gaur aptly describes Priya's strategy: "Such marriages of convenience include deception, lies and stratagems for the creation and perpetuation of a superficially secure atmosphere at home. Priya too, despite her infatuation with B.R., is careful to keep her marriage intact. She seldom displays her real self to her husband and is watchful to convey the image of an ideal wife, ideal cook, ideal housekeeper and ideal host."[7]

Priya's diary exposes her relationship with B.R. to Suresh. But Priya does not repent her action. She tells Suresh point blank that whatever she had written in the diary about B.R. and herself was true. She honestly expresses her feelings for Suresh: "if you think I ever had, or could have had, any sentiment except . . . no, not hatred, you're not even worthy of that . . . if you think I could have had any sentiment for you except ridicule—then you are just an egotistical fool; I've lived with you like a whore because you paid for it." (125)

Suresh was shocked and hurt. He told Priya to go and stay with her brother in Bombay. Priya resisted as she felt sorry for her outburst but Suresh would not listen as he told her that separation for a while would give them time to think about the matter. On reaching Bombay, she felt lost in the vastness of the city and loneliness troubled her. But re-reading of Rebecca made her feel betrayed and the revelation upturned her system of values. She realized: "I am an Indian woman," I told myself, "and for me my husband is my God." (137)

She wrote piteous letters to Suresh begging his pardon and dreamt of him in her troubled intermittent sleep and found him to be gallant, handsome and brave. She even tried to send telepathic waves as she needed his love. She also read Cheiro's Palmistry and found that it foretold a long and happy married life. On not receiving any response from Suresh, she made two unsuccessful suicidal attempts. In the first attempt she gulped down thirty Calmposes and in the second attempt tried drowning in the sea but the sharp bite of a jellyfish turned her back. She reached B.R.'s house, the ecstasy of her love for him once again overtook her for a short while. After a brief telephonic talk with Suresh who permitted her to return home, she felt a surge of joy.

Although Priya refused that she did not fantasize, it is observed that she indulged in fantasizing frequently. Her husband was not "cut of the cloth of Romance" (22) and was busy with his clients. Priya's temperament facilitated her indulgence into the world of fantasy. Her favourite author was Daphne du Maurier and favourite novel was *Rebecca.* She also read silhouette romances and often was lost in the world of mushy romance of Mills and Boons. At times she herself confessed that she "felt like a fairy godmother." While going through her mother's old books and her favourite novel *Rebecca*, she abandoned herself to the fantasies of her youth. Through her fantasies she kept her bond with B.R. intact as she herself admits that her favourite fantasy was with B.R. At night her fantasy would break all the shackles: "Sometimes I became Paro, and sometimes I was myself. Sometimes I was B.R. devouring Paro, and then B.R. tenderly loving Priya, and then I became Suresh who was ravishing Paro, and then Paro with Suresh in slavish possession and intermittently Suresh copulating with Priya who was actually Paro. I was all these people, fragments of their thoughts, feelings, terrors passed through my writhing body." (60)

Fantasy is thus an essential aspect of Priya's character. It is the means for her to attain all that which is unattainable in real life. Through fantasy she could keep contact with B.R. who was someone else's husband. Even though she was a married person, it was the vehicle by which she could acquire what she desired.

Priya's endeavours in her marital life qualified her to be called emancipated modern woman who had tried to break the shackles imposed by male-dominated society. But, like Paro, she also longed to look for something deeper, something higher than her sensual pleasures. A reply to be written to the letter sent by Mary, her friend, led her to write a confessional diary "which eventually became this novel." (120) Priya always considered herself to be a person of little consequence and less talent but now she had discovered hidden instincts in her: "I discovered, however, that I had an instinct, a faculty, for truth. I saw things as they were, not as they should have been or people tried to pretend they were. It was this faculty for truth that had haunted me for years,. distorting the happiest moments of my life, mocking love, happiness, security." (12)

The diary which she starts writing about "passion, boredom, vanity and jealousy" (144) provided her an escape route. It had a cathartic effect. In the end she comes back to her husband. Thus Priya led an inconsistent but eventful life.

B.R., the sewing machine magnate, was in *Paro: Dreams of Passion* the first lawful husband of Paro. Priya, his secretary and all the other girls working in his office loved him madly. For them he was a dreamboat. Priya narrates the condition prevalent in his office: "I was B.R.'s secretary at that time, all of us at the office thought he was a real dreamboat. He looked straight into our eye—he knew all our first names—he was a compulsive nymphomaniac." (1)

B.R.'s office was like the temple of Pallas Athene for all those working there. He had decorated the office himself where everything was perfect. All the female workers in his office felt heartbroken when they heard about his marriage with Paro. Even Priya was hurt.

B.R. possessed a compulsive passion to sell himself. His passion for women had a history behind it. He was sent to Oxford by his father against his mother's and his own wishes. He hated Oxford and India. Although he was a successful businessman yet he was not happy. He did not complain. He said: "I don't really seek or deserve more happiness than I have already got. As for womanizing, I love women; I always have and I always will. I've never paid for a woman in my life. I've never been to a whore or a prostitute! And I'm proud of it." (104)

Priya noticed "a frustrated homemaker hiding behind the lady killer image." (144) His unhappy life prompted him to run after sex. It was like a vocation, a duty for him. It was the means to reach the outer world for him. For woman he was a healer and a succourer. He never refused women. Priya tells: "Sex had become, to him, more than a sport, it was a duty, a vocation, a calling. I sensed that it was with sex alone that he reached out to the world, and it was with sex that he shut out thought, emotion and feeling. Women could, perhaps, sense this immense sexual generosity, and came to him for succour and healing. And he allowed himself to be used as a lamp-post, or as a letterbox for women to send messages to their husbands through." (40)

But he himself felt insecure and longed for love, for which he needed beautiful women who, he admitted bitterly are incapable of providing that love. He also repented marrying Paro, as he realised that she had married him out of her selfish motives. He expressed his sorrow in one of his intimate moments with Priya: "I should never have married Paro," he said. "It wasn't me she wanted. It was the fixtures and fittings that came with me. She hurt me by trying to use me." (38)

Later, he married Bubbles just six months after Paro had left him. In his opinion Paro was one of the crudest, most castrating and selfish women. He considered Priya to be as real as his mother for which he loved her and showered tenderness upon her. Apart from his womanizer image, B.R. was a meticulous businessman, a genius at marketing. The company founded by his father flourished under his regime due to his tireless efforts. Priya tells: "B.R. was a meticulous businessman, an exacting perfectionist, and almost the nervous housewife in his finicky adherence to routine and detail. He had also, I am told, a near-genius for marketing, and the company, founded by his father, flourished under his tender ministrations. He was forever wooing the Market, visiting agents, distributors, 'wheeling about,' as he wryly put it, "to charm the Dealers to do the dealing." (15)

Although he was a womanizer and a successful businessman yet, he had a desire to liberate himself from the responsibilities. He questions Priya if her book can liberate him: "My author friend, can you in your book liberate me from the onerous responsibility of making love to every attractive or unattractive woman who uses me like a dildo to make her husband jealous? Can you liberate me from the financial burdens of alimony? Can you free me from the jealous possessiveness of the one woman I love? Can you bring up my children for me?" (144) Thus B.R. is one man in private life and another in public. Though he took liberty with women in his domestic life, he managed his business efficiently.

In *Gods, Graves and Grandmother* Ammi, a Muslim Kothawali was thrown out of her Kotha. She finds herself without money in the Delhi slums where she raises a jhuggi. Her positive outlook on life and her innate resourcefulness enable her to set up a makeshift, ramshackle temple under the peepal tree behind their jhuggi. Gudiya tells us how she built up the shrine: "When my mother went away, my grandmother and I were left to fend for ourselves. I had always been given to believe that we had once been enormously rich, but at that time we were on the very verge of penury. We would indeed have starved had not my resourceful grandmother stolen a marble slab from the building site behind our shanty. This marble—clean, cold and veined with the merest hint of green shadows—she placed beneath the holy peepal tree which shaded our little hut. Then she found five rounded river stones, purloined them, really, from a sahib's rockery, and arranged them on the marble altar and our shrine was complete." (1)

Even though Ammi was a muslim, she acted as the Pujarin of the temple, collecting the proceeds of the temple, the offerings made by the devotees. As she belonged to the family of singing prostitutes, she used her liquid and mellifluous voice for singing bhajans. People were enthralled and thus turned into devoted bhaktas who did not hesitate to make the offerings. She abandoned her burka and consigned it to her trunk along with the sequined gharara and beaded reticules. Although she was not well-versed in the higher tenets of Hinduism, she quickly took to bhajan singing and often uttered with ease "Arre Rama, Rama, Rama." (12) When Gudiya asked her from where she learned the songs, she replied expressing her opinion on religion: ""In my mother's lap," she replied, "in her lap, just as you are sitting in mine."' (13)

Ammi by sheer grit and determination which are necessary components for survival, constructs a make-shift temple and converts it into commercial establishment. Being practical and not the one to shed tears, she overcomes all the obstacles of life. The first obstacle comes in the form of Sundar Pahalwan, who was a 'dada' and had territorial rights over a stretch of pavement. On this pavement was Ammi's jhuggi. He asked Ammi for his hafta of ten rupees a week. Grandmother, who had now assumed an entirely different persona, replied: "Arre Rama, Rama, Rama," she exclaimed, her honeyed voice taking on a new texture altogether. "Seize our money, Pahalwanji, but spare our self-respect. I am the widow of a Brahmin, my husband was a priest, guard your tongue or else a virtuous woman's curses may follow you!" (12)

Sundar Pahalwan was shocked by these words but being a dada of the area, he had to maintain the hold over the people. Hence, in an uncertain tone, he asked the grandmother for his hafta. She told him to come the next week and take his cash. But the following Monday Sundar Pahalwan was surprised to see Ammi singing a bhajan in front of a statue of Durga, sitting on a tiger, under a glittering canopy made from gold and red gharara. Worshippers assembled around the shrine. Sundar Pahalwan was completely overpowered and left eleven rupees in the thali before leaving the shrine. Similarly, when the man from the Municipal Corporation came with the demolition order for the "pucca cement structure" (13) where Ammi and Gudiya stayed, he fell at Ammi's feet, and begged her forgiveness for the blasphemy.

There also comes a time when Ammi's fingerprints are found on the axe with which slum-dweller Saboo had killed another slum-dweller, Shambhu. Ammi was taken to the Police Station but the presence of her devotees succeeded in getting her out of the case. Gudiya admitted that Ammi "had a well-acquired knowledge of how to handle men." (18) Even Pandit Kailash Shastry, a scholarly person, well-versed in religious rituals, accepted Ammi as his superior in religious and spiritual matters. This was achieved by Ammi by resorting to 'silence' and 'vague generalization.' Once when Pandit Kailash Shastry objected to the temple resembling a doll's house and not being built according to vastu shastra, she replied with her usual vague generalizations: "'It is all Lord Krishna's leela," she said obscurely, her garbled speech adding a further veneer of wisdom to her words: "Sab guddi-gudde ka khel hai!'" (67)

Gudiya tells us that her grandmother had perfected the art of presenting confusing abstractions as exalted philosophy and was successful in converting her lack of specific religious knowledge into gnostic strength. Pandit Kailash Shastry was so much influenced by her that at one stage, he says: "I can sense that she is an extraordinary woman with remarkable siddhis," he told Lila and Phoolwati, "If even the dust from her mind were to settle on an ordinary mortal like me, I would become a better and cleverer person." (58-59)

Pandit Kailash Shastry thus gives the status of 'saint' to Ammi. According to Sharad Shrivastav: "Ammi uses her show of 'virtue' and her 'silence' to successfully manipulate the male-dominated society. She handles Pandit Kailash Shastry by her silence and vague generalizations about theology and Sundar Pahalwan by her show of virtue and piety."[8]

With the help of Phoolwati, Sundar Pahalwan and Pandit Shastry, Ammi was able to turn the temple into a commercially viable venture. She administered the temple with iron hand. She wanted everything to be perfect. The premises were kept clean, the inner circle of devotees were assigned different tasks for the smooth running of the temple. If somebody tried to fiddle with the accounts or take home the offerings; she would immediately catch the culprit and rebuke him. Having achieved her aim of eking out a livelihood, Ammi gradually increases her 'abstraction,' 'detachment' and 'inexplicable remoteness' thereby lending a mystical charm and aura to her personality. This leads to her death being described as attaining maha-samadhi by voluntarily relinquishing her consciousness to the larger universe. She was buried in the temple premises in the lotus position. Ammi's character can be best summed up in the words of Subhash Chandra: "There is a business-like practicality about the old woman which enables her to come to grips with insurmountable troubles that dog her and her grand-daughter's life. Ammi is presented to us not only as a person who (economically shattered though she is) makes a success of her life in a highly competitive world, but also she is shown reaching spiritual heights which few women are known to have attained in or outside of literature."[9] In Ammi, Namita Gokhale created a woman who would never accept defeat. Ammi displayed presence of mind whenever occasion demanded.

Gudiya is the narrator of the story, *Gods, Graves and Grandmother*, which she tells in the first-person with frankness and candour and often in a brutally straightforward manner. Gudiya was left in the company of her Ammi after her mother ran away with a beggar. She called her mother 'her wicked waylaid mother.' (28) She had inherited pale-gold skin from some Afghan or phirangi customer of her mother. Hence she did not know who her father was. She develops along the lines in which a good-looking, ambitious and careless slum girl generally develops.

At the age of eleven, she was admitted to St. Jude's Academy for the Socially Handicapped. It was a good mission school. Prior to this she was exposed to an itinerant schooling in the form of one nursery and one municipal school. After admitting her to the school, grandmother did not take further interest in the matter and hence she attended school in a very casual manner and did what she liked as nobody bothered about her. Although she attended school casually yet she had a desire to become rich and famous. When Malvika Mehta, her new teacher, entered the school, her entire appearance and attitude aroused an instant and unprovoked hostility in the mind of Gudiya. She represented everything that Gudiya wanted to be but could not. As expressed by Gudiya, the new teacher "was extremely good-looking. She had creamy white skin, jet-black hair, cut in a short, extremely fashionable style, and a lascivious mole poised over her succulent lips. She was dressed in simple clothes that I suspected of being very expensive. Something about her looks, her clothes and her air of total control aroused my instant and unprovoked hostility. She represented everything I most wanted to be and almost, but not quite, was." (124)

When Malvika Mehta summons a group of girls including Gudiya for a counselling session and asks everyone what they would like to achieve and why? Gudiya answered that she was going to become a film star and marry the prime minister's son. She would be the richest woman in the world and travel by aeroplane. This, she thought, was possible because her Ammi had taught her that anything was possible if one aspired. But as Sharad Shrivastav points out: "The route to success through education does not appeal her. Her admission to Roxanne Lamba's English-medium school does not inculcate any higher ideals in her, nor does she have any desire for an impressive career. She can never associate success with studies—in fact, she has abhorrence for all kinds of education. The easiest course for such girls is to use their body to achieve their goal."[10]

Gudiya was quite conscious of her beauty and body. Since her adolescent stage she was beginning to realize that she was beautiful and this thought exhilarated her. She desired to enter the world of glamour and excitement, a world which was unknown to her and which she associated with her absent mother. Although she wondered what must be the ultimate end of her mother's romances, yet she wanted to be outrageous and wicked like her.

Gudiya despised her name because she didn't feel like a doll. So she resolved to change her name, her identity, her very self. After a lot of thinking, she changes her name to Pooja Abhimanyu Singh. As she had no idea who her father was, she had wide scope for imagination. Sometimes she imagined herself to be the daughter of an English Lord or an Arab Sheikh or a passionate blue-blooded bandit who was shot dead after secretly marrying her mother. But she finally settled on the chance discovery of a discarded photograph of a noble-looking man with a waxed moustache to be her father. The new name acquired by her brings a change in her. It makes her more confident, poised and graceful, the hint of which we get when she confronts Mr. Lamba, Roxanne's husband, and Cyrus, her nephew, regarding the will left by Roxanne Madam.

Following the footsteps of her mother, Gudiya falls in love with the young handsome, orphan, bastard, bandwallah, a member of the Shiv Mohan Band party. He was named Kalki, the scourge of the Kalyug by Pandit Kailash Shastry. Her infatuation for Kalki was so intense that she does not hesitate to establish relationship with him. She does not even bother to know about his name, parentage or past. The result of this was that Gudiya becomes pregnant and Phoolwati, with the help of Sundar Pahalwan, forces Kalki to marry Gudiya. It was necessary that the unborn child must have a father so that he would not be called an illegitimate child. After marriage, Gudiya was disappointed with Kalki's behaviour and wondered what she had seen in him. Phoolwati also advised Gudiya not to waste her time with the bandwallah as their purpose of giving father's name to the unborn child was over: "The child will have a legitimate father now. Your Kalki has served his function. You can't waste your life like this, Gudiya, with these bandwallahs!" (216)

After a few months of an unhappy married life, and the cruel treatment from Kalki, Gudiya feared that her life would pass in indifference, indignity and calculated cruelties. However, the advice of Phoolwati and conversation with Lila serves as an impetus for Gudiya to take decision. She sold her ornaments and bought a one-way ticket to Bombay for Kalki, gave him some money and packed him off to Bombay, so that he could try his luck in film industry. After Kalki's departure, Gudiya accepted the past and decided to live in the present along with Phoolwati and Mallika, her daughter.

Gudiya shares excellent rapport with Phoolwati. It was Phoolwati who gave her support when Ammi became indifferent towards her. When Gudiya's menses began, Phoolwati explained her about womanhood. She brought a length of ribbon, a set of bindis, a small mirror, a kajal stick, even a bright, shiny lipstick for Gudiya. She was overcome with gratitude and resolved never to forget Phoolwati's kindness. After Ammi's death Gudiya stays with Phoolwati in her house. She would even write letters to Sundar Pahalwan on behalf of Phoolwati. She also lent emotional support to Phoolwati when Sundar Pahalwan was dead.

Gudiya has a close association with the peepal tree under which her grandmother had built the temple. The peepal tree was the presence in their lives. Its leaves talked to Gudiya in a sibilant murmur. The peepal tree prevented Gudiya from having a clearer knowledge of the unspeakable act between Shambhu and Magoo and her mother and Riyasuddin. The frenzied clapping of the leaves, as they whispered and whistled feverishly to each other, obscured that vision of these acts. The peepal tree rebuked Gudiya when she took out one gold guinea from grandmother's trunk by shrieking at her. But every night as she fell asleep, it would begin its seductive song. Even when she went to stay with Phoolwati after grandmother's death, the peepal tree carried with it million slumbering presences. She visited the tree after a long time with Phoolwati and Sundar to dig the gold coins, Gudiya knew that the million slumbering presences were all safe in its branches.

Gudiya's character has another trait, that of fantasizing. The fantasy of peepal tree with slumbering presences is recurrent. These presences had become her friends: "Every night, as I fell asleep on my folding cot near the window, the peepal tree would begin its seductive song. Shutting my eyes tight against the visions, I would still encounter the energetic acrobatics of Shambhu and Magoo, of my mother and Riyasuddin Rizvi. There were other ghouls and spirits who dwelt in that peepal tree, a man with a blank featureless face, no eyes or nose, nothing save a large red mouth that was always laughing. And then a sad polite lady who was always sighing and who smiled apologetically whenever she caught my eye. Except for my mother and her friend, and Shambhu and Magoo, none of them ever mocked or frightened me." (28-29)

When she fell in love with Kalki she fantasized him in her dreams. She along with him would dance around trees in a filmi manner. His eyes blazed intensely. She would spend time fantasizing about Pooja, her background, her family, her past and her future: "I decided that Pooja had been switched at birth by a careless hospital attendant. The other child, the actual Gudiya, was growing up, surrounded by comfort and luxury, in her ancestral home. Her doting parents complied with her every wish, little realizing that she was nothing but a changeling, while the real Pooja Abhimanyu Singh languished in Phoolwati's hut, deprived by cruel fate of her true heritage." (144)

Gudiya's character is rather unfortunate. She had to live without maternal affection and paternal protection. Though she dreamt of marrying a rich and influential person, she ended by marrying a bandwallah.

Phoolwati in *Gods, Graves and Grandmother* was the widow of Shambhu, the Bihari giant who owned a tea stall. She came to Delhi after the death of her husband. She had come for the inquest and funeral of her husband but decided to stay on. She was plump and attractive woman with the most enormous bosom. She had a better head for business than her husband and had a commanding personality. We get the glimpse of this when Gudiya tells us: "Although she had never previously left her village in District Madhubani, Bihar, she knew precisely what she was about, and before we knew it she had negotiated a reduced five-year rental from the street-lord Sundar Pahalwan, with a percentage of the take thrown in." (26)

Phoolwati took charge of her husband's business and expanded it. She also diversified the business and set up another stall just outside the temple which sold incense and marigold garlands and coconuts and little brass amulets which she had ordered from Moradabad. She also got done the coloured postcards of Ammi with 'Om' printed across them in gold-embossed lettering and sold them for two rupees each. She did not spend time mourning her husband's death but faced the world boldly. She even became the trusted lieutenant of Ammi, handling her cash and no major decision in the temple was ever taken without her.

Phoolwati was courageous and handled Sundar Pahalwan very tactfully. He became mild in front of her. When he saw Phoolwati while she was returning from temple, he blushed and smiled at Phoolwati. On the other hand Phoolwati was not afraid of him. She justified being called an avatar of Durga by Ammi. She faced the Pahalwan boldly and questioned: "Lost your tongue?" she said sharply. "Such a Dara Singh bulk of a man, but with the courage of a mouse! Why are you so scared of Phoolwati, man? Will she bite you? Will she eat you up? Arre bhai, Phoolwati is just a timid woman, and you are a hero-wrestler. Just say what you have to say. You want to discuss business with me, don't you? Then say so! Come to my house at seven this evening, and we can discuss whatever you want to!" (105-6)

Sundar Pahalwan becomes Phoolwati's partner in her various enterprises as well as her life. But before accepting the marriage proposal she puts certain conditions before him. First he would build a pucca house for her, the ownership of which would be hers. Secondly, she would continue her business and thirdly, Gudiya should be treated as their adoptive daughter. Sundar readily agreed to all these conditions.

Phoolwati never lets her grip on Sundar Pahalwan become loose and at times she even scolded him. Once when Bhimsingh, Roxanne's chauffeur came to take Gudiya, Phoolwati got annoyed and scolded him. Sundar Pahalwan also threatened him and lifted him by his collar suspending the chauffeur in air. Gudiya scolded Sundar Pahalwan and asked him to put the man down. Phoolwati also changed her stand and scolded Sundar Pahalwan who was completely taken aback: "You joker, I called you here at seven, and instead you stroll in any time and beat up my guests? Just who do you think you are, Mr. Wrestler?" (108)

Sundar constructed a pucca two-storey building with all modern amenities for Phoolwati. No expense was spared in its construction. It had even more marble than the temple. Phoolwati furnished her dream house with the help of Gudiya. Sundar was amused but did not grudge the enormous expenses. He was the most indulgent husband and took efforts to keep Phoolwati happy. He was always full of effusive praise for Phoolwati. He says affectionately: "I tell you, Gudiya," he said fondly, "no one in the whole of India can match my Phoolwati for brains. M.A., B.A., Ph.D.—she is cleverer than all that. If they made my Phoolwati the prime minister of India, she could solve all the problems of this country." (191)

After the grandmother's death, the evening bhajans at the temple continued but sometimes problems were faced in the playing of tape recorder. These problems would have affected the number of devotees visiting the temple. Pandit Kailash Shastry suggested that discourses from the *Bhagavad Gita* should be delivered by him to retain the interest of the devotees. Phoolwati objected and suggested that she would sing the bhajans. She started learning music. Although she lacked musical talent yet she made her debut in singing: "Phoolwati made her debut. From the moment she picked up the mike, she was a star. Her infectious smile, her energy, her optimism, her spontaneity, all communicated themselves to her audience." (122)

She did only stop at this. Next she started picking up popular film tunes and adapted the lyrics to religious sentiment. For example, 'Mera naam chin chin choo' became 'Mera naam, main Shivji hoon.' Her bemused audience quickly got hooked and even Pandit Kailash Shastry had to admit that the songs went down better than his discourses.

Phoolwati was a good administrator. When Ammi died, the number of devotees thronging the temple increased. These devotees had to be handled tactfully and patiently. The task was assigned to Phoolwati who handled the situation remarkably well: "Phoolwati's, administrative talents shone before the challenge. Each visitor to the temple was presented with a coloured picture postcard of Ammi, along with a piece of coconut and small card which proclaimed: 'Blessings from the Motherhead.' There were orderly lines and neatly cordoned queues, and something about Phoolwati's substantial presence prevented the scores of distraught mourners disintegrating into a riot." (81-82)

She also exhibited her dynamism and confidence when she encountered Mr. Lamba and Mrs. Roxanne regarding Gudiya's future. She dealt with them on equal footing without being self-conscious about her economic and social status, Gudiya noticed: "Something in her encounter with Roxanne had clearly struck a deeply competitive chord. This was a completely revamped and re-upholstered Phoolwati. She wore an expensive silk sari, patterned in yellow and purple. A thick gold chain festooned her plump neck and a patent leather handbag was slung about her shoulders. A new-found poise seemed to have accompanied these sartorial changes, and her already abundant confidence had transposed into a cool assurance." (92)

Another important aspect of her character is her affectionate and cordial relationship with Gudiya. She took the responsibility of Gudiya whole-heartedly. Phoolwati's presence in her life gave her stability. It was Phoolwati who introduced Gudiya to the magical world of films. She brought for Gudiya her first ice-cream and gave rudimentary outline of the facts of life. It was Phoolwati's cheerful presence which gave an edge of reality to the strange existence of Gudiya and Ammi. Gudiya asserts the role of Phoolwati in her life: "Phoolwati's dignity, intelligence, perseverance and goodwill gave a stability and bulwark to my young self. We shared the same fiercely independent spirit, but mine had floundered in the confusion of identity and norms. Whatever or whoever I had lost in mother and grandmother I regained in abundant measure in Phoolwati's love and warm embraces, and her flatulence and mammoth bosom bothered me not a bit." (57)

Phoolwati, with the help of Sundar Pahalwan, compelled Kalki to marry Gudiya. It was she who urged Gudiya to return to her house sensing Gudiya's condition after marriage. She supported Gudiya and her daughter after Kalki had left to try his luck in Bombay. She treated Gudiya as her adopted daughter. The relationship between the two was very fond and loving. She would tell Gudiya: "Arre, Gudiya, you are born to be a princess—you have your grandmother's blessings. Tell Phoolwati what you want, Gudiya, and she will get it for you. Just test your Phoolwati for once." (162)

Phoolwati was fond of cooking. The food she prepared was usually oily, spicy and extravagantly flavoured. She suffered intensely from the problem of gases. She would contort her body to improbable postures to ease its passage. She would coax it out through a burp or a belch. It seemed that eternal spring of 'vayu' resided in her. When she was taken for task for this, she would say that the bhoga was the most difficult part of yoga.

Phoolwati was very hostile towards Lila, a disciple of grandmother. She would call her 'that buddhi' or 'Ekdanti' as she had a single protruding tooth. She tried all means to get rid of her from the temple. On the other hand she was sympathetic towards the three lepers who begged outside the temple. Ammi had developed hatred for the beggars and all forms of beggary and hence disallowed the beggars to sit outside the temple. Phoolwati secretly gave some money and old laddoos to them. She told Gudiya not to tell this to her Ammi. She had done this because her mother had taught her to give alms to the poor. According to Subhash Chandra: "Phoolwati's association with Ammi, her say in the matters of the temple and her quick earthly responses in not only seizing the opportunities but also creating them, establish beyond doubt her capability as a courageous, practical and farsighted individual, not given to maudlin reactions, but with a healthy practical perspectives on life which enable her to survive, prosper and carve a niche in the new surroundings into which she is thrown on account of Shambhu's sudden death."[11]

Phoolwati's character is beautifully portrayed by Namita Gokhale. She is practical and faces the world boldly come what may. Hostile circumstances do not deter her from her path towards emancipation.

Parvati in *A Himalayan Love Story* grew up in Jeolikote, a popular tourist halt located on the way to Nainital. She lived with her widowed mother in two rooms perched above a small kirana shop, having lost her father when she was one year old. The house was provided to them by her mother's step-brother, Hiranand Joshi who was the Principal of a school in Nainital. Parvati's mother, being a poor widow, was reluctant to give education to Parvati but on the insistence of her brother had no other option than to accede to his wishes. She considered it a waste of money and would say that it would have been better if she were a boy so that he could earn and provide for her old age: 'She would complain bitterly about the cost of books and uniforms, although the actual school fees were of course heavily subsidized. "It would be different if you were a boy," she would say angrily, "then you could earn and provide for me in my old age. But all you are going to do is get married to some no-good and take my gold Champakali necklace off with you as dowry. It is a double curse, to first be born a woman, then get straddled with another female to provide for."(6)

Although Parvati's mother had not to provide for her upbringing as the rent of the shop was adequate for their meagre requirements, Parvati aspired to become rich. During her childhood days, it was her duty to collect firewood for cooking food. Along with the wood she would collect pine cones and stored them in the little shack beside the outdoor privy. On being asked by her mother about the collection she replied: "I'm going to build a palace of pine cones. We can even live there. It will be warm and cozy in winter, and if I paint the pine cones golden everyone will think we are very rich." (13) In return for this answer she received a slap from her mother, but being a stubborn person she continued with her collection of pine cones. She resolved to have the world's largest collection of pine cones and make some sensible use of it. This would make her mother repent for her action and then she would forgive her.

Parvati was not surprised when she found her mother in the arms of Shrikrishnaji, the kirana shop owner. There was no way she could find the truth and hence decided that although her mother and the woman with Shrikrishnaji looked similar yet they were two different people. She even went to the extent of thinking that her mother was possessed by some spirit and decided not to confront the spirit or else she would die. When her mother had high fever she nursed her devotedly and wondered if her illness was the result of her shameless spying on her mother. She feared that the spirit had found out and decided to destroy her mother.

Parvati had the ability to recognize the masked faces of people. She would look at other's faces, at their expression of laughter and sadness and wondered at the ease with which they carried these masks. She felt a sense of anger and unease. She began at a very early age to avoid people. Her world was shattered when she found her mother drinking liquor along with Shrikrishnaji: "People were not as they appeared. There was another life behind their masks. These cavorting figures were no better than ghosts—they belonged to a nightmare. I shut my eyes tightly, willing them to disappear, but they were no wraiths, my mother and our tenant stood before me in the flesh, their true nature unmasked." (16-17)

When Parvati fell in love with Salman Siddique, the history teacher, she immediately sensed that he wore a mask, the knowledge of which excited her and she took the challenge of establishing relationship with him. Salman's beauty had dazzled Parvati and soon she started pestering masterji for help with her history homework. Masterji tried his level best to clear her doubts but ultimately told her to get her doubts cleared from Salman. Had Parvati's mother been alive she would have disapproved of Parvati being taught history by a young man. Salman was more interested in establishing relationship with Parvati than teaching history. Parvati knew that she was playing a shadow game and both were well aware about the fact that the passion was not a permanent one. Hence when Salman left Parvati without even bidding goodbye, the rejection didn't hurt her. She could bear the pain.

At this juncture Masterji fixed marriage of Parvati with Lalit who was also her friend and was a Brahmin like her. Masterji had done his duty and now it was Parvati's turn to do her duty. Hence the question of rejection did not arise though she was attracted towards Mukul Nainwal. Marriage with Lalit was not a happy one as Lalit was a homosexual and therefore could not fulfill the marital duties. He was hostile towards Parvati and she wondered whether the roots of this hatred had started establishing itself in those happy days at Wee Nooke where she had been bonded in friendship with Mukul and Lalit, giving her safety and security: "After our marriage, after I became Mrs. Lalit Joshi, I realized that the stubborn hostility that Lalit harboured towards me could not have developed overnight; it had its roots in those happy days at Wee Nooke: he must surely have hated me even then. Gradually, this hatred seeped osmotically into my system, and became both a verdict and a sentence." (34)

It was Mukul's visit to their house in Bareilly, where they had shifted, which made Parvati realize that she had blundered her way into a nightmare. Lalit's look at Mukul with hunger and lust changed the course of life for Parvati. In Mukul's pleading eyes she could see a question that demanded no answer but an absolution. It was in his eyes she found her answer. She had to abide by the codes set for a married woman: "I was a Hindu woman, a married woman. I would tenaciously live out the role, safe in its stern unremitting code. If I performed the motions with enough fluency and ease, then perhaps within the confines of my neglected womb, I would find the inner space, the private territory, the strength to stage and execute a very private revolt." (37)

Parvati does not succumb to her aroused desire for a long time. She would cook and smile and wear her new frozen face which she was condemned to wear for a long time with perfection. Her silence was thought to be praiseworthy reticence which was normal to the Indian woman. This silence was broken by the arrival of Lalit's younger brother Raju, who was different from him in every way. There was optimism and panache in his attitude which attracted Parvati. Raju, on finding Parvati sleeping in the kitchen, was not least surprised. Soon they grew friendlier to the extent of establishing physical relationship. Parvati considered Raju to be an ally and felt safe in his company although she could sense that she was heading towards a terrible and inevitable fate. But she was optimistic that one day she and Lalit would lead a normal married life: "I cherished the secret hope that, one day, we would have a normal marriage. Lalit was, after all, my husband. He earned for me, I cooked for him; we had been friends in our childhood. We could become lovers, confidantes, allies." (44)

Penury had trained Parvati and she took charge of Masterji's household when she went to stay with him in Nainital. She was also good at culinary skills. She took delight in preparing most elaborate meals for Lalit. He enjoyed the food. Parvati took satisfaction in the praise showered by Lalit's family members also. She felt safe when Lalit ate the food cooked by her. She felt that she exercised some power over his body and his house. She often pictured Lalit coming home with gajra of mogra flowers and beautiful sarees for her. Parvati started loving Lalit but his death due to T.B. shattered her dream of a happy married life. She nursed Lalit through his disease and even tried to arrange money by sending letters to Masterji and Mukul so that she could keep him in Bhowali sanatorium for treatment. But before posting the letters Lalit had died.

Parvati was expecting a child at the time when Lalit died. This was the outcome of her relationship with Raju. She returned to Wee Nooke where the trouble began. Sometimes she would weep and sometimes she would scream. The doctors could not understand what she was saying. She was desperately in need of her mother but she was not there to comfort her. By the time she gave birth to her baby, she had gone insane and was ultimately lodged in a mental asylum at Bareilly. Parvati was well aware of this doom since her childhood. She had encountered a mad woman when she had gone to collect firewood. She was dressed in rags with dirty and uncombed hair. Parvati had not seen anybody so frightening in her entire life. The woman cautioned her that, although then Parvati was young and pretty which once even she was, very soon she would become just like that mad woman. This encounter had terrified Parvati and she could sense her doom: "The terror of that afternoon has remained coiled in my heart, and through every action of every hour of my life, I have been aware of it. That was the day I realized I was doomed. I had nothing to gain in life, only to lose. I would become like her. My hair would fall off, and my teeth as well, for her madness had called out to mine." (15)

Parvati is the product of circumstances. Orphaned at an early age and dependent on her unmarried uncle, she accepts the life as it comes. She does not openly protest against the treatment meted out to her by her homosexual husband but stages a silent rebellion.

Mukul in *A Himalayan Love Story* is the childhood friend of Parvati and Lalit and is the narrator of the second part of the novel. He returns to Nainital after receiving a letter from Hiranand Joshi from Hong Kong, where he worked for the International Relief Organization. Hiranand Joshi was proud that despite his handicaps Mukul was financially best settled and had moulded himself in the image of a 'Gentleman' as desired by him. In his letter he wrote: "Of all my protégés, it is to you alone that I can entrust the sum total of my Life's intellectual and material endeavours (paltry as they are) and I know you will not have pre-deceased me." (54)

Hiranand Joshi was confident that Mukul would not betray his trust and therefore after much consideration he decided to leave his cottage, Wee Nooke and orchard near Bhowali and his library consisting of 375 books in the care of Mukul. He was fully confident that Mukul would put to some constructive use all these things. He wished that all his life's belongings should be used for the upliftment of the hill folk or for the purpose of education. Mukul could not resist as he owed his present life to Hiranand Headmaster.

Mukul found this, a fine opportunity to return home as the unrequited love for Parvati which was since long forgotten was also beckoning him to return. He returns to Nainital with an ecstasy of a school boy going home on a holiday. He experienced the feeling that his youth had returned. On his way to Nainital, he found every landmark echoing his memories:

> Every landmark had a corresponding echo in my memories. Here I had passed, at fourteen, on my first visit to the plains, full of hope. And then, heartbroken after her marriage, I have travelled this same dusty road, in my new official jeep, to meet Parvati and her husband Lalit in Bareilly.
>
> Lalit was dead now, and Parvati insane. I had loved them both. These were not passing memories, nor were they daydreams. Older and wiser, I was at last returning home. (66)

Parvati was the only woman Mukul loved. But she was married off to Lalit, his friend, who was also a Brahmin like Parvati on Hiranand Headmaster's behest. Mukul had told Hiranand Headmaster about his love for Parvati before leaving for Allahabad. Hiranand Headmaster, through a letter, expressed his doubt whether Parvati would be suitable for Mukul as his partner and within a week he settled Parvati's marriage with Lalit. Mukul, later expressed his feelings to Irra: "Your grand-uncle Hiranandji, who has left me this house now—he was the same man who prevented me from marrying your mother! He wouldn't allow me to marry her. He mated her to that tubercular Lalit instead because his genes were right." (104)

This hurt had been lingering inside Mukul for a long time, almost a quarter century and took the form of an outburst. He had never felt inferior just because he was a Khasiya Brahmin. Although his grandfather was just a Phulariya Brahmin he knew that his grandfather was a Thuldhoti, a Pant from Uparora. He never revealed this fact to Hiranand as he was too proud and too certain that caste would not be a matter of concern for a person like Hiranand who read G.B. Shaw, Bertrand Russell and Rabindranath Tagore. But what hurt him most was the rejection of Parvati, when she said in one of the conversations that she could have never married Mukul. He forgave Hiranand

Headmaster for his letter but he could never forgive her tone in which she had said it. It was a wound which he nursed with devotion.

Although hurt by Hiranand Headmaster, Mukul fulfilled his ambition of becoming a moderately successful man. Mukul, a fatherless boy received private tuition from Hiranand and in return Hiranand used him mercilessly as his spy. Mukul would be the first to tell him about the happenings in the school. As a reward he would be lectured on Honesty. Everyone in the school hated him. He received the title of 'the collaborator' and the boys used him to tease Hiranand Master. He was also tortured by the boys in school. Mukul never expressed the pain he experienced. As he says: "I never told Hiranand Headmaster of the pain his attentions caused me. I remained pathetically grateful for the occasional communicative look, the private pat, the sharing of information and opinion, the belief in future, the mere sanctuary of a home." (120)

His stay at Allahabad for further studies opened new avenues for Mukul. He felt relieved from the shadow of being Hiranand Headmaster's collaborator. Here he discovered the dizzying joys of camaraderie. He made friends and enjoyed in their company. He had by now started hating Hiranand but his hatred never reflected in the letters written to Hiranand. He strived to fulfil Hiranand's ambition and asserted himself to be a very successful man. He thought that Hiranand had chosen to love him because he himself was an unloved one.

Mukul gets married to Adeleine, the widow of a French diplomat, whose photograph she wore in a gold locket. She was the daughter of a Burmese doctor and her mother was a Britisher. Mukul and Adeleine did not have their own children and he thought that Adeleine's daughter from her first marriage, was a little too modern for him. On seeing Parvati's daughter Irra he felt that she could have been Parvati's and his daughter. He considered Parvati and Irra to be his personal responsibility but when Adeleine calls him back, he returns agreeing to the settlement planned by Jeevan Jaundice and Irra.

Mukul is also a tool in the hands of circumstances. He loved Parvati but could not marry her. On the behest of Hiranand Headmaster, he comes to Nainital but is unable to do something constructive.

Rachita Tiwari, the narrator of the novel *The Book of Shadows,* had sought refuge in a lonely hilltop bungalow located in the Himalayan retreat of Ranikhet after her lover committed suicide and his sister threw acid at her. She was trying to re-invent her zest for life in that lonely bungalow. The house was not unknown to her as her mother belonged to the mountains and as a child she had spent many happy summers in the house which belonged to her Mamaji. She was confident that the hills would help her to hide and forget the past.

Here in the house she made an attempt to sustain her pain. She had left behind the world and stayed in the house with Lohaniju and the Bhotiya dog Lady. She found Lady to be the last link with the living world who kept her sane. She experienced an absolution from pain and salvation, when Lady licked her by soft furry tongue. She struggled to remain sane as she was all alone struggling to regain her self. She used various means to keep herself sane. She kept a close watch on her sanity and was alert on the signs which indicated that she might collapse.

Rachita tried to associate herself with various things which she felt would assure her sanity and help her sustain in this world. She thought of taking care of her nails. The process involved giving them perfect oval shape and painting them pink, which was the colour of love rather than red which was the colour of violence. Perhaps she felt that would help her sustain another day. She even got busy reading the noted Hindi poet Mahadevi Verma's poetry. She sought help of poetry which she once despised. She was drawn to Mahadevi Verma's poems as moth is drawn to candle. She identified herself with Mahadevi, the poet of shadows, who too lived in those hills and died there in an old house facing the snow mountains

She was constantly in the flux of uncertainty for which she took the help of an old school arithmetic book. She spent time completing the simplest sums, which gave her delight of certainty and predictability. She covered her scarred face with a chiffon dupatta beneath which she felt cocooned, private, and anonymous. She avoided social interactions as she was unable to handle them. She ultimately realised that the only anodyne for her pain was the path of self-discovery. She asserts: "If you lose—if one loses—one's sense of self, there is no remedy but to proceed on a simulated model. All self-image is anyway a construct of circumstance. If you lose an arm or a leg, you cannot forget what you have lost, the phantom pain is there to remind you, but if you have lost your sense of selfhood things are quite different, for (this is the important part) you are no longer there to know it. Who will find you again?" (216)

Nature also plays a vital role in her quest for self-discovery. Once when she went for a walk, she stumbled over a branch of pine. She had to clutch the nettle bushes to avoid falling on her face. Holding the stinging leaves for support, she understood: "There was a lesson in that, a lesson I understood instantly. The nettles are the natural guardians of the mountains, they resist intrusion and prevent the soil they grow upon from being desecrated. A firm hold on anything, even reality, hurts less than a timid half-way encounter. Pain is a precondition to life, a prelude to joy. It is a teacher, not a tormenter. Lack of stimulation leads only to a lack of sensation. Better, then, the pain." (70-71)

Whenever she experienced the emptiness within, she was made to realize by nature about her right to exist. The splatter of the rain and the dawn made her aware that she was the part of creation. Her waking up after the sleep was also her awakening to the reality. She experienced the sudden insight into her innocence, her lack of culpability and her exoneration: "When dawn broke I felt all right. I felt as though I had the right to exist, as though I was a part of creation, of the dawn chorus, of the healing sunlight that was showing up in shy dappled patches in the garden. I was a glob of consciousness, of reactions and conditioning, enveloped in skin (damaged skin, but nevertheless). I was defined in time and space and dimension, I had the right to exist! That was the breakthrough, the sudden insight into my innocence, my lack of culpability, my exoneration." (212-13)

That morning when she awoke from a night of rain-drummed dreams, she experienced the moment when the ordinary became extraordinary, when mind and body were graced by some redeeming joy. She felt as though some passing angel had graced her with the gift of forgetting and purged her of the pain. She looked into the mirror for the first time after those agonizing months. She saw her face, and she realized that she looked just fine. She had become thinner than she used to be. Thereby her face looked better and her shoulder length hair left loose covered up her damaged face. She realized that with slight makeup she could face the world again.

The deep disturbances in her self-image and the sense of depersonalization that were dogging her simply vanished and she was her self again. She does not deny succumbing to the pressure and guilt. She had convinced herself that her body which loved warmth and celebration was the culprit. It did what it shouldn't have done and in return paid the price. She also felt that it was not her body that betrayed her but it was she who had betrayed the body by abandoning courage: "It is not my body which has betrayed me—it is I who have betrayed this body. My abandonment of courage has been no less treacherous than Anand's. Courage is not simply a virtue—it is the testing point of all virtues at the highest conflux of reality. I will not fail this test of courage—I will venture unafraid into the future, with my body, with my mind, with my spirit." (219)

Rachita realized that to be oneself one must remain in control of one's life. We must make and remake ourselves, possess and repossess our world, cast and recast our lot in all previous moments. We must know what to hold and what to discard. This self-realization gave her a feeling of being alive. She felt as though she had acquired and possessed herself again. She experienced the excitement of rebirth. Earlier her world was reduced to anarchy and chaos, but now it had reintegrated itself. It dawns upon her: "Pain is a habit, pain is an orientation. It can be repudiated. It can be left behind. This house that has taken me in, where I have let loose my fears, hidden my shame—this house which has nurtured and healed me—is it now at last time to bid farewell to this house?" (230-31)

Rachita derived confidence and sustainability from nature. She felt that as long as the hillside, the snow-mountains would last in this uncertain world, she would also remain. All the activities of nature would proceed as usual and Rachita felt that she would also sustain life. Nature was always there to support her. Thus, Rachita fights her own battle. Instead of taking support of human-beings, she derives strength from nature to live on.

Shakuntala, in *Shakuntala: The Play of Memory* was the daughter of a widow. She grew up in mountain country. Her father, a Vaidya, died when she was barely five years old. His absence remained a stark presence in their unsheltered life. Her mother learnt from her father the art of healing. The smell of mountain herbs and the odour of milk and dung of the two cows which they tended always clung to her. Shakuntala loved the cows but while milking them feared that she would carry the same odour as her mother. She would run away to play in the garden outside her home. Her mother tried to impart her the meagre knowledge she had about the medicinal plants but

Shakuntala resisted the attempt with anger: "I hated everything about my mother, from her tangled hair to her shuffling gait and her cracked, dirty feet, I did not ever want to become like her." (8)

Although Shakuntala hated everything about her mother and did not want to become like her yet she loved her mother in her own stubborn manner. Her spirit and mute courage served as an impetus to the challenges confronted by Shakuntala. Long before her mother died she had forgiven her for her nagging, her unspeakable partiality to her brother, Guresvara. She swallowed the pain and jealousies like a bitter potion, a medicine which strengthens. In spite of that she provided comfort to her brother against the fear of demons.

To escape from the bondage of her situation, Shakuntala was eager to get married. She believed that girls were of no use to merit the caste or varna. Only after marriage she could rise to the gotra of her husband. Soon she was wedded to Srijan, a mahasamant, much older than her. Their marriage was soon in trouble when she discovered that she can't conceive. Further Srijan brought from one of his travels, a handmaiden. This betrayal, Shakuntala had not anticipated. During her childhood she used to get angry when her mother favoured her brother over her but this betrayal was the worst: "I had known rage before, and anger, when, as a child. But this was worse, a collapse of all that had been good and true in my life. I screamed and sobbed aloud, beating my head against the stone walls of the temple like the kind of woman I had not imagined I would ever become." (58)

Whenever Shakuntala was confronted with problems she would seek isolation by running away from home, ponder over the situation and hide herself from shame. She felt safe and even secure in her despair and loneliness. She was ready to forgive her husband who was a soft and kind man. She was sure that he would send back the handmaiden, whom she blamed for this situation. She found no fault in her husband: "My husband had not hurt or scorned me. He had brought a woman home from his travels to work as my maid and do my command, but she had looked down at me from a great height and viewed me with contempt. It was not his fault." (59)

Shakuntala was hungry for experience and had a quest for knowledge. As a child this desire unfolded itself when she wished she were a kite which could flutter in wind and view all the lands below. There were things which she wanted to see, to know, to do, because her ignorance irked her. Her marriage to Srijan had made possible what seemed impossible. Shakuntala then moved on as a straw in the ocean of her compulsions. She called herself Yaduri and went off with a Greek traveller.

For her now, the world was a wild and wondrous place. She experienced gladness in her freedom and traversing the world with the Yavana, Nearchus who had seen and known much. She observed: "I was hungry for knowledge, as a bear for honey. The Yavana did not scorn my curiosity, he did not think it inappropriate of me to ask so many questions." (135)

Together they travelled far and wide and surrendered to unbridled pleasure. They reached Kashi, the destination that Shakuntala had always ached to arrive at. They had to stay in foreigner's quarters which were located on the other side of the river. Shakuntala adjusted herself to the changed circumstances with ease. Although she arrived in the city of her choice yet she stayed as an outcaste. She would imagine the antiquity and the splendour of Kashi: "From the window I saw the great sweep of the heaven-river and the majestic temples on the far shore rising into the sky. Kashi: if it did not exist, the gods would have had to invent it. I was at last in the city of my imaginings." (140)

But being surrounded by foreigners who talked in strange language, Shakuntala soon felt unsettled and restless. Her mind wandered into past though she tried to resist it. She was now filled with regret when she thought of her husband Srijan. She compared her condition with Kalidasa's Shakuntala: "Even in the moment of her disgrace, Kalidasa's Shakuntala had the sanctity of a secret marriage. But I had betrayed everything. I had renounced my name, I was no longer Shakuntala, only Yaduri, the unmentionable one. I had abandoned the husband whose true wife I was. No matter that he had other wives before me. The noble king Dushyanta had wives aplenty, and yet there was no slur in his love-making with Shakuntala. The apsara Menaka, whose daughter Shakuntala was, had seduced the great sage Vishwamitra—but then she was an immortal, and such deeds are permitted to nymphs and celestials. Only I stood condemned." (150)

Shakuntala missed the mountains where she belonged, even the Ganga appeared to her as slower and without music in those flat and dull plains. She thought herself also to be different. She was not the one who sat beside Srijan and drank the sacred Soma wine or the one who would listen to the difficult wisdom of the fisherman with whom she conferred when she was agitated. This was another Shakuntala, who knew no reproach as her destruction was inevitable. She was the woman without recourse and was kept away from the holy city like the Yavanas. She realized that the cords that connected her to her body had been snapped. She was filled with remorse: "My body has abandoned itself to shame here. It hungers, lusts, contorts with pleasures that grow weaker and more desperate by the day. Darker, and more pitiful. Somewhere, the cords that connect me to my body have snapped. This could be anyone's body; I watch it with horror and a certain fascination. I am nobody; I am a body. A traveller picked me up as he might pluck a fruit from a tree, and now he is impatient to throw the core away." (161)

There was a time when Shakuntala would have staked anything to gain experience but now her appetite for experience was no longer strong. She realized that although one might travel for many nights and days, one belongs to the place from where one began: "The place where one began was perhaps the only place where one belonged. My friend, the fisherman Kundan, would have understood my predicament. As I lay in that room, surrounded by sounds and smells and people I did not know, I longed above all to be at the abandoned temple, by the hidden passageway where the oil lamp flickered, where the vision of a strong and beautiful goddess had once blessed my fears." (172)

Driven by the urge to go to the real Kashi, Shakuntala left Nearchus one fine morning without his knowledge. She asserted that she was a strong woman, a mother of unborn child and set out unafraid. She reached Kashi where, while straying in one of the lanes, she was attacked by the charging bull. Shakuntala was wounded with a torn womb. She was looked after by a Buddhist Renunciate who, during the course of treatment, told her to embrace the Buddha but her stubborn spirit would not yield. She could not embrace the Buddha just to please the nun. Seeing death hovering over her, she reminded herself that she could not surrender yet. She had to return home to Srijan. She felt that it was not from him that she had run away but she had set out in search of a part of herself, the part which had eluded her. She thought that dying in the holy city of Kashi was a blessing but she had not willed it so: "I would not depart humiliated from these shores. I would hide, escape, return to the earth and the rocks that knew me, and the parrots, and the patient fisherman who sat by the banks of the Ganga, baiting her fish." (198)

With an unfulfilled desire to return to the mountains, her home, Shakuntala, the eternal outsider, the wife who does not belong, the whore who was ruled by shame eventually sought redemption.

Thus we find that Namita Gokhale has created characters in her novels which will linger in our minds long after we have read the novels. In her novels one finds oneself in a world dominated by women characters, with male characters existing as supporters and performers of secondary roles. We have, Paro and

Priya in *Paro: Dreams of Passion* seeking self-fulfillment, self-assertion and having an ambition to liberate themselves from the patriarchal set-up. Ammi, Gudiya and Phoolwati in *Gods, Graves and Grandmother* display grit, courage and determination to face all the odds of the society. They carry on with their lives without the male support and end up as emancipated beings.

Parvati in *A Himalayan Love Story* tries to adjust in the given circumstances. She seeks freedom through sexual autonomy. She is depicted as fragile, stubborn and hungry for justice, adventure and good fortune in an unjust, introverted and decadent society of Kumaoni Brahmin. Rachita in *The Book of Shadows*, is courageous and has the spirit to fight her own battle in hostile conditions. She seeks help of nature and the old house where she spent her childhood along with its caretaker, Lohaniju for survival and sustenance.

Shakuntala in *Shakuntala: The Play of Memory*, sees herself aloof from her life. As a girl, she is restless to see the world and to know that is unknown. As a woman she sets out on the journey towards freedom and self-fulfillment. Her attempt is thwarted by circumstances and ultimately she seeks redemption.

The male characters portrayed by Namita Gokhale are ignorant of the plight of the women they are associated with. They fail to give them support and are not assertive. They are engrossed in their own pursuits. Apart from major characters, Namita Gokhale has been able to effect the development of secondary characters like Sundar, Kalki, Lila, Roxanne, Irra, Lohaniju, Guresvara etc.

NOTES

1. Sharad Shrivastav, 'The Aberration—II Namita Gokhale,' *The New Woman in Indian English Fiction: A Study of Kamala*

Markandaya, Anita Desai, Namita Gokhale and Shobha De, New Delhi: Creative, 1996, p. 140.

2. Kuldeep Kumar and Gajendra Kumar, 'Deconstructing Femininity: A Reading of Namita Gokhale's *Paro: Dreams of Passion*,' *Indian English Literature,* Vol. I, ed. Basavaraj Naikar, New Delhi: Atlantic, 2002, p. 154.
3. Subhash Chandra, 'Female Subjectivity and Female Empowerment in the Fiction of Namita Gokhale,' *The Literary Voice,* No. 3, February 1996, p. 53.
4. Sharad Shrivastav, p. 104.
5. R.S. Pathak, 'Namita Gokhale's *Paro: Dreams of Passion* or Passion of Dreams?' *Recent Indian Fiction*, New Delhi: Prestige, 1994, p. 181.
6. Sharad Shrivastav, p. 106.
7. Rashmi Gaur, p. 181.
8. Sharad Shrivastav, p. 117.
9. Subhash Chandra, p. 17.
10. Sharad Shrivastav, p. 117.
11. Subhash Chandra, p. 17.

Conclusion

Namita Gokhale is undoubtedly one of the Indian women novelists to have depicted the predicament of women. Women in her novels emerge as individuals challenging their existential survival. Gokhale has been successful in catching the whole woman alive in terms of feelings, intellect and emotions.

Namita Gokhale poses a question to the very concept of femininity and feminism. In denying the social codes of femininity, Paro her character in *Paro: Dreams of Passion*, has tried to achieve the equality and individuality. Paro, no doubt, asserts her femininity but at the same time she does not behave in a masculine manner. The type of feminism Paro propagates is self-destructive as it does not lead to any harmonious relationship between man and woman which should be the ultimate aim of feminism.

Through Paro, Namita Gokhale has deconstructed the very concept of femininity which expected women to be docile, submissive, chaste and modest. Paro has, in fact, denied all these codes but in a very unhealthy manner. It is quite easy to discuss Paro as a 'bad' or 'fallen woman' in a casual critical appreciation of the novel. Kuldeep Kumar and Gajendra Kumar remark about deconstructing the femininity in Paro: "By reading the novel deconstructively, a perceptive reader/critic may gain new and fresh insights about its characters and events, since the deconstructive critical endeavour does not accept a label or a concept at its face value. It brings to the fore what is generally, hitherto hidden from our view. Paro, deconstructively speaking is neither a 'bad' nor 'a good woman.' She is just what she is and what she wants to be."[1]

In her novels, Namita Gokhale has narrated the efforts of the women characters for self-assertion. They face many problems and difficulties but they try to empower themselves. This forms the basis of the first chapter on Empowerment of Women. Regarding her work being women oriented, she feels a woman's life is "reflected in the rhythm of the seasons, not like men whose stories are rooted in wars, territories and legislation."[2]

Paro and Priya in *Paro: Dreams of Passion* wage a struggle for self-assertion. They revolt against the social and moral code assigned to a woman by patriarchy. Rape by the art teacher changes the course of life for Paro. She sees her body as the means to assert herself. Her marriage with B.R. is also unsuccessful owing to B.R.'s infidelity. She divorces B.R. and seeks sexual autonomy to assert herself by establishing relationship with a number of men. As Ashok Kumar observes: "With the women's awakening and with the assertion of their rights they have also asserted their right to their bodies. The female body has been a site for feminine struggle."[3]

Paro succeeded to some extent in breaking the stereotype image of women, who are thought to be in need of male protection and guidance. She confidently declared, "I depend on nobody. I am my own person." (48) She tried to achieve equality and individuality. But hostile circumstances led to her suicide.

On the other hand Priya is ashamed of her middle-class background and vows to liberate herself from her middle-class existence. She idolizes and imitates Paro. With a desire to rise above her middle-class life, she marries a successful lawyer in Delhi, and grooms him and herself towards becoming part of the social elite. She also has relationship with B.R. even after marriage. But at the end, she returns to her husband.

Ammi, Gudiya and Phoolwati in *Gods, Graves and Grandmother* are emancipated women. They confront the difficulties with courage and conviction for self-assertion. All the three are displaced but they establish firm roots in an unknown city. Ammi and Gudiya are thrown out of their kotha while Phoolwati comes to Delhi after her husband's death. Ammi builds a make-shift temple with available resources and becomes empowered. She almost attains sainthood. Gudiya desires Kalki and marries him. For self-identity and self-worth, she changes her name to Pooja Abhimanyu Singh. She soon realizes her mistake of getting married to Kalki and sends him to Bombay to pursue his dreams. Thus she liberates herself from the shackles of unhappy marriage.

Phoolwati takes over the business of her dead husband, having good acumen for business, she diversifies it and the business flourishes under her able management. She gets married to Sundar but after his death carries on with her life.

Ammi, Gudiya and Phoolwati constitute a world of women in which they seem to be modelling their own lives according to their own desires without getting bogged down by any social forces. In fact, they seem in command of the situation they face, whereas the men they come in contact with are either murdered or subdued. They seem to fulfill the matriarchal utopian vision which aims to see women as powerful with "command over their bodies and their lives."[4]

Parvati in *A Himalayan Love Story* seeks self-assertion through sexual autonomy. As a child she is witness to her mother's illicit relationship with the kirana shop owner. This has deep impact on her psyche. She experiences the first bout of lunacy. Usha Bande points out: "The fundamental benevolence of mother helps a child in developing confidence in self as well as in other. Mothers provide them with a safeguard against the onslaught of a hostile world. However, if the image of a good mother is shattered by some mischance, an individual's fear, dislike and contempt are fierce. These are in proportion to the intensity of his emotions towards the idealized good mother."[5]

After her mother's death, Parvati goes to stay with her step-uncle. She resorts to sexual freedom in search of self-identity without fearing the consequences. Her marriage to Lalit, a homosexual, worsens her condition further. She rebels silently taking help of his brother to fulfill her physical needs. Parvati's struggle ends in her madness, the seeds of which were sown when she lived in Jeolikote.

Rachita in *The Book of Shadows* makes efforts for self-assertion after an acid attack on her face. This attack disfigures her face and destabilizes her mental peace. To seek solace and isolation, she goes to her ancestral home in the Himalayas, abandoned but for an old caretaker, Lohaniju. It is nature which infuses in her the spirit of survival. Here Namita Gokhale seems to suggest that if humans fail in their duty, nature is always there to comfort, console, guide, and support the person in trouble. Nature can be the healer of pain inflicted by the humans. Rachita expresses the sudden revelation: "As I looked up at the sky, the encroaching band of darkness that had threatened the periphery of my vision for so long suddenly disappeared. I had an ecstasy of understanding so sweet that it could not possibly be true. I knew then that I had travelled to the edge of my world, and returned, and that the world was good. The stars above bathed me in their love, and an ebullient sure strength surged through my blood, pounding and panting with the excitement of rebirth." (230)

Shakuntala in *Shakuntala: The Play of Memory* is the victim of gender discrimination during her childhood. After marriage her husband, Srijan, brings a handmaiden, a betrayal which she cannot sustain. Her hunger for knowledge, experience and freedom results in her elopement with a Greek horse merchant. Here the novelist seems to suggest that betrayal by the person on whom you rely can lead to such actions which at times make you repentant. Breaking the set traditional norms, she seeks sexual pleasure. But ultimately is filled with remorse, and with unfulfilled desire to return home, dies in Kashi, the city of her longing. Her condition can rightly be described in the words of S.B. Tiwari: "Human life is suggested as a journey in quest of self-identity or emancipation from the miseries of life. But influenced by man's modernism, ego and Karma and governed by fate and chance, human life moves in a zig-zag way and at last comes to the same state from which it starts but with man's self-realization of his puny stature and the truths of life in tradition-bound social set-up."[6]

Namita Gokhale projects the predicament of women in her novels belonging to different sections of society. Shobha De has also projected the sufferings of women in her novels but of those belonging to upper middle-class society. For De, the sexual exploits are the expression of the free woman, symbol of emancipation and individuality. Namita Gokhale also holds the same view. However, she shows that where sex is a man's whole life, for a woman, it is only a secondary need—her principal concern being her identity. This identity could be that of the self as artist, in the case of Paro, or a novelist in case of Priya, to remain sane in case of Rachita or a culturally imposed role identity, as wife, mother etc. The novelist clearly establishes that for a middle-class woman, sexual dalliance is the outcome of personal involvement with a single man. Despite this, she still experiences a sense of guilt and remorse and longs for a happy life.

Namita Gokhale's Kumaoni upbringing, close association with the hills and movement in metropolitan cities have influenced her writings. Like William Wordsworth she also has the romantic recollections of the past. Her association with her past—places, people as well as nature—has been dealt in the second chapter. She has beautifully portrayed the places which she might have visited in the past. She has encompassed in her wide spectrum, places associated with not only metropolitan cities but also the hill-stations. She has fond memories about

Nainital which she has recorded in her novels. Gokhale's description of places is realistic and this realistic portrayal produces immense dramatic effect. She has the ability to cohere and analyze the whole pattern of society around her.

Her portrayals are highly informative. The characters described by her also display her keen sense of observation. The details of the exotic locales are so apt that without going there you can experience the beauty of nature.

Namita Gokhale is an artist in language. This is amply displayed in her novels. A close study into the narrative technique displays her skill in handling the language. It is found that for all her novels she has used first-person narrative mode of expression with occasional use of flashbacks. The first-person narrative enables the narrator-protagonist to present what she sees, thinks or feels. To retain the Indian touch of the novel written in English, Gokhale has used large number of Indian words without translating them into English.

Her novels are replete with wonderful descriptions displaying her observant nature. Her descriptions are lively in the true sense. To make an impression, she has used various figurative devices. Personification and onomatopoeia have made the following account appealing: "The wind had become a gentle whisper, stirring the leaves of quiescent trees, lighting their patient rugged barks as it shook the rows of circularly strung bulbs. A temple bell chimed softly in the breeze. Its sound was distinct from all other sounds, from the revelry of the fairground, the filmy music of the bioscope, the steady incantation of the priest, the crackle of the microphone, the murmur of wind. It was separate and yet it was internal to the whole." (87)

The Indian situations described in her novels are typical as well as realistic. At times she has conveyed the emotions and feelings of a character through the description of her eyes. Death scenes are also realistically portrayed.

It is observed that Namita Gokhale makes frequent experiments while handling the language to convey her point of view. In her novels we find extensive use of similes and metaphors. The comparisons give us the exact meaning which she wishes to convey. At times instead of describing the things in details, she has personified them to convey the desired meaning. Alliteration as a stylistic device is abundantly found in her novels to enhance the effect. Phrases as well as words are repeated to bring about rhythmic beauty as well as to lay emphasis on the statement made.

Namita Gokhale is fond of imagery particularly of 'animalification.'[7] She has used them to convey the mental and physical condition of her characters. She also describes attitude as well as movements through imagery. Paro in *Paro: Dreams of Passion* used "her mocking wit as adeptly as a sharp little scorpion" (32) and in *Gods, Graves and Grandmother*, grandmother after Shambhu's murder was "still and sentinent as a hooded snake" and still "as a little mongoose" (20). Kamala Markandaya has also used animal imagery in her novels. She has used imagery to hint at characters' depravity or predicament. In Gokhale's novels images are used to indicate mostly the behavioural patterns of her characters.

Gokhale has also made abundant use of symbols to provide the novels with multiple and deeper meaning. The titles of her novels like *Paro: Dreams of Passion* and *Shakuntala: The Play of Memory* are symbolic. The temple in *Gods, Graves and Grandmother* is symbolic of people's faith in things related to religion. When Panditji is predicting the fortune of Gudiya an ant was crawling over his kurta and later "had crawled all the way up his collar and was now poised on the folds of his angavastram." (140) The ant is, in fact, an apt symbol and indicates in many ways, the future course of events. Certain symbols are used to represent the desires, loneliness, attachment, struggle, love, care etc. Gokhale has used symbols to suggest certain things.

Like Bhabani Bhattacharya, Namita Gokhale has also used irony—situational as well as verbal—to expose the human predicament. As Gokhale is a minute observer of the society, she also found evil intentions of people. She neither condemns nor reacts but simply gives ironical smile on the incongruities and eccentricities of society.

Namita Gokhale exhibits a unique sense of humour in her novels. She looks for humour in all situations, often in serious moments. This is because in spite of the sufferings in her life, she admits, in an interview with Smita Khanna, that "Life is a tragedy for those who feel, and a comedy for those who think."[8] Occasional use of irony and humour adds liveliness to the account. *Gods, Graves and Grandmother* is not without humour. In fact, her humour has been often mentioned as surreal humour. When soon after founding the rudimentary temple, the grandmother "prostrated herself before the pebbles and the marigolds on the green marble slab, lay down so still and silent and for so long that" Gudiya, "was afraid she might be dead or in a coma." (2) The young woman, Magoo "succumbed to Shambhu's charms" and they were always "smiling into each other's eyes, although Shambhu of course had only one." (17)

Namita Gokhale has presented in her novels a wide variety of characters. For her: "Writing a novel is also a therapeutic experience. Human character and human destiny are formed by the way we handle our life crises. When you write a novel, in hindsight, you realize that you were actually examining why you made certain choices. But, at the same time writing is a neurotic activity. You build a parallel universe, you play God with your characters."[9]

The protagonists of all her novels are women. She has presented in her novels different shades of her characters. Like Robert Browning's dramatic monologue, she places her characters in difficult situations and then portrays their responses to such situations. Almost all her women characters struggle for self-assertion without fearing the consequences. She strongly feels: "Articulation is the first step in the process of empowerment, communication the next. The vision of Saraswati, the voice of the muse, these gifts come from the longer, larger view."[10]

As a woman writer, she is fully aware of her constraints: "All manner of scientific and technological advances are usurping women's biological role as perpetuators of the human race, leaving them gloriously free to be human beings. Yet, even today, when women write as women, they often write not in their unique voice as a fragment of creative consciousness positioned to view an endlessly expanding horizon. They write instead as victims of biology, gender and circumstances, from within the bars, as it were."[11]

Paro in *Paro: Dreams of Passion* is presented by the novelist as the seductress. She is the product of her circumstances. Her only fault is that she fails to rise on the occasion and succumbs under the impact of factors which are beyond her control. The treatment that she received from her parents and at the boarding school was painful: "Every relationship and encounter seemed to have ended in bitterness, misunderstanding and wrangling." (29) She at times breaks the conventions to assert herself. Priya is stunned by her choice of person like Shambhu Nath Mishra. But the life like that in a fairyland cannot be perpetuated for ever. R.S. Pathak opines: "Like any exhausted gross sensualist, Paro is ultimately doomed to suffer from an atrophy of emotions and cynicism."[12]

She tried to take life in her stride. At times she resorts to exhibitionism and to play-acting in a desire to know herself. But disillusioned with her life, she commits suicide. As Rashmi Gaur rightly points out: "However even an uninhibited Paro finds it impossible to nullify the social conditioning and is haunted by the contradiction which generations of mental, economic and emotional slavery have fixed in the feminine mind. Even she is not able to take on the world as a sovereign arbiter of her own destiny."[13]

Priya is a foil to Paro and presents a different aspect of a woman's voyage to self-identification. As a middle-class girl she is influenced by the charm and sophistication of B.R. and bold beauty and reckless charm of Paro. She longs to resemble Paro and makes every attempt for it. She has an affair with B.R. and is happy in his company but her marriage with Suresh and the later development made her really miserable. Her lawyer-husband is busy in his own aspirations and has no time for his wife and her real needs. Her marriage does not provide her love and happiness. The two factors which were chiefly responsible for Priya's estrangement from her husband are: the abortion of her child and her husband's knowledge of her relations with B.R. The bond between her and her husband having severed, the relation between the two became tense. But after a brief separation from Suresh, she comes back to her husband and marriage.

B.R. makes an indelible impact on the women he encounters. He marries Paro and has relationship with Priya. B.R., who is a victim of satyriasis, a form of sexual intensity, can be said to suffer (in terms of Jungian psychology) from the "masculine mother-complex."[14] He strives to seek his sexual counterpart with the help of an "inherited collective image of woman in his unconscious."[15] Apart from what he is in his personal life, he is a meticulous businessman, a marketing genius, under whose able guidance his father's company flourished. Through the life and experiences of the three main characters in the novel the novelist has tried to convey a message to the readers. She seems to suggest that a life of unbridled sexual indulgences is not the solution to life's challenges.

In her novel *Gods, Graves and Grandmother*, Ammi after being thrown out of her kotha displays her innate resourcefulness when she establishes a temple in Delhi slums. She is not afraid of any eventuality whether imposed on her by fate or men. Gudiya, her granddaughter, on finding how miserable her life had become with Kalki, sends him to Mumbai. Although her Ammi had taught her that anything is possible if one aspired, her desire to lead a glamorous life remains unfulfilled. With grandmother dead and Kalki gone, she leads her life with her daughter and Phoolwati.

Another character, which is effectively portrayed by Namita Gokhale, is of Phoolwati who comes to Delhi after her husband's death. She successfully handles his business. She tackles Sundar Pahalwan tactfully and becomes his partner in various enterprises merely due to her fearlessness and determination. She has solutions to all problems whether of Gudiya or the temple. She is a good administrator. Like Daniel Defoe's Moll Flanders, Phoolwati too, is aware that in a mercantile society, the marriage market is heavily biased in favour of men. Hence, to pre-empt any such move from Sundar Pahlawan's side, Phoolwati gives her consent to marry him subject to the conditions laid down by her. As Sharad Shrivastav observes: "In the milieu of Phoolwati the 'conditionalities' if at all, would come from the male side, but here we find Phoolwati reversing the prevalent norm of the society. She is not an avowed feminist but her practical common sense, view of things coupled with her domineering stature, do bring about this reversal of roles."[16]

Parvati in *A Himalayan Love Story* is again a product of hostile circumstances. Her age, family background (with a tubercular mother and austere anglophile Uncle Hiranand Joshi) and times go on to shape her as wind shapes a rock. Without anyone to guide here, she tries to assert her identity by establishing relationship with her history teacher. She is attracted by Mukul, her friend but is unable to convert it into a marriage.

After marriage with Lalit, she enters into relationship with his brother, gives birth to his daughter and becomes a lunatic in the end. She is unable to sustain the burden of troubles.

Rachita in *The Book of Shadows* flees from her agony to the hill resort of Ranikhet. Here she tries to re-invent her zest of life without the support of anyone. She fights her own battle. She struggles to remain sane and regain her self. It is nature which helps her in her endeavour. She at times meditates on her thoughts only to become aware of the fact that one must remain in control of one's life. The book has been a cathartic experience for Namita Gokhale. She comments about the end of novel as well as the end of Rachita's journey: "Initially, I had thought that at the end of the novel, Rachita would go back to the city, perhaps have a plastic surgery and live on. But somewhere along the way, I realized that this wouldn't happen. She would live on in that house in the hills. This is symbolic of my living on in the world of—well, I won't say psychic because I mock the obviously psychic—let's say, in the world of the spirit."[17]

Shakuntala in *Shakuntala: The Play of Memory* is hungry for knowledge and experience for which she seeks freedom. She is subjected to gender discrimination by her mother. She regards marriage as an escape as well as an avenue to rise above the existing status. She receives love from her husband initially but he betrays her. This provokes her to rebel and run away with an unknown Greek horse merchant. Here Gokhale seems to suggest that betrayal from the person you deeply rely on can lead to a revolt which does not think about the implications and consequences. But in the end she realizes that one belongs to the place where one began. Her desire of returning to the hills is thwarted by her tragic death.

It is to be noted that Namita Gokhale, like D.H. Lawrence, has openly discussed sex in most of her works. But they cannot be easily termed as pornographic. They have some fine images and symbols, words and phrases which make them appealing to the connoisseur of art. In art, it is not the matter but the manner that matters. Shobha De and Arundhati Roy have also dealt with sex in their novels but Namita Gokhale has referred to sex more artistically. Freud, a great psychologist, has expounded a highly revolutionary theory of sex. So now sex is not a taboo but a part and parcel of life. Namita Gokhale asserts: "In India, too, women's voices moved out of the hushed silences of upper middle class drawing rooms into the real world, with my own first novel Paro being a case in point, followed by Shobha De and other users of the genre. This considerably franker attitude to sexuality was the core issue in articulating a more real and honest consciousness in the face of conservative and hypocritical society."[18]

A thorough study of Gokhale's novels shows her perceptive portrayal of secret depths of the human psyche. Her captivating style invokes vivid images and compels the reader to identify himself or herself with the characters and situations. She has tried her best to expose the moral and spiritual breakdown of modern society in which a hapless and forsaken woman longs for pleasure and wants to fly freely in the sky of freedom. Though she has been severally criticized by the champions of ethics and morality, her novels are all fine pieces of poetic and metaphoric exactitude which haunt our mind long after we have read them.

Namita Gokhale's novels constitute a broad, encompassing feminist vision which visualizes a rightful place for women in the patriarchal society. She wants women to be self-sufficient for living with self-respect. She needs to be applauded for her effort. On account of her keen concern for women, peculiar style of presenting her views and re-creation of the life she experienced, Namita Gokhale has ensured for herself a prominent place among the Indian women novelists in English.

NOTES

1. Namita Gokhale, "Glimpses of Kumaon: An overpowering obsession with the hills," *India Today.*
2. Ashok Kumar, "Women Empowerment through Indo-Anglian Literature," *Critical Responses to Feminism*, ed. Binod Mishra. New Delhi: Sarup, 2006, p. 29.
3. Kuldeep Kumar and Gajendra Kumar. "Deconstructing Femininity: A Reading of Namita Gokhale's *Paro: Dreams of Passion*," *Indian English Literature*, Vol. 1, ed. Basavraj Naikar, New Delhi: Atlantic, 2002, p. 157.
4. Jyotsna Agnihotri Gupta, "Feminist Utopias—Strategies for Women's Empowerment," *Gender and Literature*, ed. Iqbal Kaur, New Delhi: B.R., 1992, p. 40.
5. Usha Bande, "Mothers and Mother-Figures in Anita Desai's Novels," *Critical Studies on Indian Fiction in English*, ed. R.A. Singh and V.L.V.N. Narendra Kumar, New Delhi: Atlantic, 1999, p. 32.
6. S.B. Tiwari, "Old Wine in New Bottles: Traditionalism in R.K. Narayan's Novels," *R.K. Narayan: Reflections and Re-valuation*, ed. Chhote Lal Shastri, New Delhi: Sarup, 2006, pp. 26-27.
7. Don L.F. Nilsen and A.P. Nilsen, *Language Play*. Mass: Newbury, 1978.
8. Namita Gokhale, interviewed by Smita Khanna, "Nawab, Kawab and Behanji," *Times of India,* 24 July 2006.
9. Namita Gokhale,.http//www.lifepositive.com.
10. Namita Gokhale, "Gender and Literary Sensibility," *Indian Writing in English: The Last Decade*, ed. Rajul Bhargava, New Delhi: Rawat, 2002, p. 67.
11. *Ibid.*
12. R.S. Pathak, "Namita Gokhale's *Paro: Dreams of Passion* or Passion of Dreams?" *Recent Indian Fiction*, ed. R.S. Pathak, New Delhi: Prestige, 1994, p. 181.
13. Rashmi Gaur, "Paro: A Tale of Two Ladies," *Women Writers in the Twentieth Century Literature*, ed. Monika Gupta, New Delhi: Atlantic, 2000, p. 178.

14. C.G. Jung, *Four Archetypes*. London: Routledge and Kegan Paul, 1986 rpt. p. 19.
15. C.G. Jung, *Aspects of Feminism*, London: Routledge and Kegan Paul, 1982 rpt. p. 79
16. Sharad Shrivastav, "The Aberration—II, Namita Gokhale," *The New Woman in Indian English Fiction: Study of Kamala Markandaya, Anita Desai, Namita Gokhale and Shobha De*. New Delhi: Creative, 1996, p. 115.
17. Namita Gokhale, http//www.lifepositive.com
18. Namita Gokhale, p. 65.

Bibliography

Abrams, M.H. *A Glossary of Literary Terms*. New Delhi: Akash Press, 2007.

Agnihotri Gupta, Jyotsna. "Feminist Utopias—Strategies for Women's Empowerment," *Gender and Literature*, ed. Iqbal Kaur, New Delhi: B.R., 1992.

Alam, Qaiser Zoha. "Namita Gokhale's *Gods, Graves and Grandmother*," *Indian Writing in English*, ed. Manmohan K. Bhatnagar, New Delhi: Atlantic, 1998.

Anand, T.S. "Paro: A Psychological Approach," *Indian Women Novelists*, ed. R.K. Dhawan, Set II, Vol. VI, New Delhi: Prestige, 1993.

Bande, Usha. "Mothers and Mother-Figures in Anita Desai's Novels" *Critical Studies on Indian Fiction in English*, ed. R.A. Singh and V.L.V.N. Narendra Kumar, New Delhi: Atlantic, 1999.

Beauvoir, Simone de. *The Second Sex*. Trans. and ed. H.M. Parshley, 1953; rpt. Harmondsworth: Penguin, 1983.

Bharucha, Ferheiz C. "Namita Gokhale's *Paro: Dreams of Passion*: Meaning through Mediocrity" *Indian Woman Novelists*, ed. R.K. Dhawan. Set II, Vol. VI, New Delhi: Prestige, 1993.

Bhatnagar, Manmohan K. *Indian Writing in English Vol.I* , New Delhi: Atlantic,1998.

Bhattacharya, Arnab. "Bitter-Sweet Memories," *The Telegraph*, June 10, 2005.

Chandra, Subhash. "Female Subjectivity and Female Empowerment in the Fiction of Namita Gokhale," *The Literary Voice*, No. 3, February 1996.

_____."The New Woman in Namita Gokhale's *Gods, Graves and Grandmother*," *Indian Women Novelists*, ed. R.K. Dhawan. Set III: Vol. 6. New Delhi: Prestige, 1995.

Derret, M.N. *The Modern Indian Novel in English*. Brussels: University Library, 1996.

Dhawan, R.K. *Explorations in Modern English Fiction.* New Delhi: Bahri, 1992.

Forster, E.M. *Aspects of Novel*. London: Edward Arnold, 1945.

Friedan, Betty. *The Feminine Mystique*. 1963; rpt Harmondsworth: Penguin, 1971.

Gaur, Rashmi. "Paro: A Tale of Two Ladies," *Women Writers in the Twentieth Century Literature*, ed. Monika Gupta, New Delhi: Atlantic, 2000.

Gokhale, Namita. *Paro: Dreams of Passion*. Chatto and Windus, The Hogarth Press, 1984.

_____. *Gods, Graves and Grandmother*. New Delhi: Rupa, 1994.

_____. *A Himalayan Love Story*, New Delhi: Har Anand, 1996.

_____. *The Book of Shadows*. New Delhi: Penguin India, 1999.

_____. *Shakuntala: The Play of Memory*. New Delhi: Penguin India, 2005.

_____. http: //www.lifepositive.com

_____. "Glimpses of Kumaon: An Overpowering Obsession with the Hills," *India Today*.

_____. "Gender and Literary Sensibility," *Indian Writing in English: The Last Decade*, ed. Rajul Bhargava, New Delhi: Rawat, 2002.

_____. "Nainital," *The Penguin Book of Indian Journeys*. New Delhi: Penguin India, 2001.

_____. On her book "The Book of Shadows."

Gordon, Linda. *Feminism and Recent Fiction in English*, ed. Sushila Singh, New Delhi: Prestige, 1991.

Gupta, R.K. *The Novels of Anita Desai-A Feminist Perspective*, New Delhi: Atlantic,2002.

Iyengar, K.R.Srinivasa. *IndianWriting in English,* New Delhi: Sterling,1985.

James, Henry. *The Writer and the World*, ed. Leon Edel, London: Rupert Hart Davis, 1957.

Jung, C.G. *Four Archetypes*. London: Routledge & Kegan Paul, 1986.

_____. *Aspects of Feminism*. London: Routledge & Kegan Paul, 1982.

Khanna, Smita "Nawab, Kawab and Behenji," *Times of India,* 24 July 2006.

Kreisber, Nadine. "Difficulty pushes us to fight, to grow," *Indian Express*, 22 July, 2007.

Krishnaswamy, N., et.al. *Contemporary Literary Theory*. New Delhi: MacMillan, 2001.

Kumar, Ashok. "Women Empowerment through Indo-Anglian Literature," *Critical Responses to Feminism*, ed. Binod Mishra, New Delhi: Sarup, 2006.

Kumar, Kuldeep and Gajendra Kumar. "Deconstructing Femininity: A Reading of Namita Gokhale's *Paro: Dreams of Passion*," *Indian English Literature*, Vol. I, ed. Basavraj Naikar, New Delhi: Atlantic, 2002.

Mukherjee, Meenakshi. "An Area of Brightness," *The Week*, 26 July 1996.

_____. "The Problem of Style," *The Twice-Born Fiction*. New Delhi: Arnold Heinemann, 1971.

Myles, Anita. *Feminism and the Postmodern Indian Women Novelists in English,* New Delhi: Sarup, 2006.

Neb, N.K. "Feminist Stance in Shobha De's Novels," *Critical Responses to Feminism,* ed. Binod Mishra, New Delhi: Sarup, 2006.

Nilsen, Don L.P. and A.P. Nilsen. *Language Play*. Mass: Newbury.

Pathak, R.S. "Namita Gokhale's *Paro: Dreams of Passion or Passion of Dreams?*" *Recent Indian Fiction*, ed. R.S. Pathak, New Delhi: Prestige, 1994.

____ "Indianization of English: Language and Literature," *Indianization of English Language and Literature*, ed R.S. Pathak, New Delhi: Bahri, 1994.

Prasad, Amar Nath. *New Lights on Indian Women Novelists in English*, Vol. I , New Delhi: Sarup, 2003.

Quraishi, Humra. "Every book has its life, its Kundali," *The Tribune*, Sept. 15, 2002.

Ramamoorthi, P. "My Life is my own: A Study of Shashi Deshpande's Women," *Feminism and Recent Fiction in English*, ed. Sushila Singh, New Delhi: Prestige, 1991.

Reddy, Sunita Y.S. *A Feminist Perspective on the Novels of Shashi Deshpande,* New Delhi: Prestige, 2001.

Rao, Raja. *Kanthapura*. London: George Allen and Unwin, 1968.

_____. 'The Writer and the World,' *The Literary Criticism*, Vol. VIII, No. I, Winter, 1965.

Sherril, Anne and Paula Robertson Rose. *Four Elements: A Creative Approach to the Short Story*. New York: Holt, Rinehart and Winston, 1975.

Shrivastav, Sharad. "The Aberration—II Namita Gokhale," *The New Woman in Indian English Fictions: A Study of Kamala Markandaya, Anita Desai, Namita Gokhale and Shobha De*. New Delhi: Creative, 1996.

Singh, Kanwar Dinesh. *Feminism and Post Feminism: The Context of Modern Indian Women Poets Writing in English,* New Delhi: Sarup, 2004.

Singh, Khushwant. "A Woman of Talent and Guts," *The Tribune*. Oct. 30, 1999.

Singh, Sushila. *Feminism and Recent Fiction in English*. New Delhi: Prestige, 1991.

Singh, Veena. "Woman as Portrayed by the Women Novelists of India," *The Brown Critique*, No. 10-12, Oct-Dec 1995.

Singleton, John. "The Writing Self," *The Creative Writing Workbook*, New York: Palgrave, 2001.

Varghese, Paul. *Literary Criticism—A Workbook*, Madras: Macmillan India, 1981.

Sorot, Balram. *The Novels of Bhabani Bhattacharya*. New Delhi: Prestige, 1991.

Tiwari, S.B. "Old Wine in New Bottles: Traditionalism in R.K. Narayan's Novels," *R.K. Narayan: Reflections and Re-evaluation*, ed. Chhote Lal Khatri, New Delhi: Sarup, 2006.

Uma, Alladi. "Women and Her Family," *Indian and Afro-American—A Literary Perspective*. New Delhi: Sterling, 1989.

Venkataraman, Janaki. "Arrested Flight" *Indian Review of Books*, 16 Dec. 1994-15 Jan. 1995.

Wellek, Rene and Austin Warren. *Theory of Literature*. London: Penguin, 1949.

